Badges
of the
Canadian Navy

Badges

of the
Canadian Navy

J. Graeme Arbuckle

NIMBUS PUBLISHING LIMITED

Published by:
Nimbus Publishing Limited
P.O. Box 9301, Station A
Halifax, N.S. B3K 5N5

Typesetting: McCurdy Printing & Typesetting Limited, Halifax

Printed in Hong Kong by Everbest Printing Co. Ltd.

Design: J. W. Johnson

Copyright to Badges reproduced here is held by The Department of National Defence and Maritime Command.

Information regarding individual Badges is taken from **BRCN** 150 and **CFP** 267, Maritime Command Museum, Admiralty House, CFB, Halifax.

Canadian Cataloguing in Publication Data

Arbuckle, Graeme, 1953
    Badges of the Canadian Navy
Includes index.
ISBN 0-920852-49-1

1. Canada.   Canadian Armed Forces.   Maritime
Command—Medals, badges, decorations, etc.
I. Title.
VC345.A72 1987   359.1′4′0971   C87-090077-3

Table of Contents

DEDICATION

To the men and women of the Canadian Navy whose service to crown and country preserves freedom and peace.

Preface

As the Canadian Navy prepares itself for the rapidly changing technologies of the future, it is fitting that this book on Naval badges should be published, for in its pages is to be found a wealth of information about the Navy of the present and an excellent picture of the great heritage upon which the Canadian Navy has been built.

The ship's badge is one of the many honourable traditions upon which our pride in our Service is built. The badge carries the name of the vessel, the motto and the battle honours through generations of sailors brought together in allegiance to the ship, the Navy and the country. The importance of the ship's badge as an outward and visible sign of an inward spirit and cohesion cannot be over-emphasized.

This book, however, is not just about ships. I am proud to see the badges of the Naval Reserve Divisions, the Naval Air Squadrons and the shore establishments included, for each has played a distinctive role in our Navy's heritage and each is destined to play an important role in its future.

This book should be required reading, not only for the serious naval historians but also for the mildly curious who will glean much information from these pages about the history of individual units, their names, mottoes and battle honours.

Ready Aye Ready.

> Fred J. Mifflin
> Rear-Admiral
> Deputy Commander Maritime Command

Badges of the Canadian Navy
Introduction

This book of badges complements an earlier book, *Customs and Traditions of the Canadian Navy* (1984 Nimbus), which describes naval lore and the origins of the structure and formalities of the navy. One of the most colourful facets of this rich heritage is the pageantry of flags, pennants and especially badges — distinctive emblems for ships, air squadrons, reserve divisions and shore establishments. The badges come directly from the long-standing traditions of the Royal Navy and the official recognition and subsequent development of them in the first half of the twentieth century — from 1909 to the present. In Canada the badges were not given their officiality until 1948.

These badges are symbols of allegiance and represent the name, the origin and sometimes the function of each vessel. As graphic devices of identification they conform to the requirements of any badge, but are more elaborate and individualistic than some devices. The rationale of a badge originates in the context of combat where easy recognition of friend and foe is vital. Symbols, or badges, have been identified on shields, armour, flags, pennants, ship's castles and so on, from earliest times. Badge and crest are two terms that are frequently confused. According to Iain Moncrieffe:

> A crest is the personal device of its owner; it is borne on a helm and is part of his achievement of arms. A badge on the other hand is a distinctive emblem borne separately from shield and crest as a mark of allegiance, ownership or dependence, and today is often used to indicate membership of an armigerous body.[1]

The elements are of course interchangeable, as for example in the case of the fleur-de-lis which was used as part of the royal coat of arms of England and can be seen as a universal symbol for France and the province of Quebec. In this collection there is one personal badge, that of the Commander, Canadian Fleet.

Canadian naval badges demonstrate a number of directions that can be taken in constructing a two-dimensional representation of a name. Since a large percentage of these vessels are named for a city, township or province the badge designer has been able to use elements from an heraldic device associated with the name. In the example of HMCS *Saskatchewan*, this is an original Canadian source — the wheat sheaf from the provincial coat of arms, but another direct but distant source is seen in HMCS *Digby* where the ostrich is taken from the crest of William, 5th Baron of Digby, father of the Hon. Robert Digby, Rear-admiral of the Red, Commander-in-chief in North America (1781-1783) in whose honour the town is named. This gives an authentic heraldic connection. *Digby* also demonstrates how the function of a vessel, in this case a minesweeper, is incorporated in the badge, for the gold disc symbolizes a mine. Other directions are more inventive. Take *Antigonish* for example, a Micmac word to describe a place of broken branches, the site of this Nova Scotia town. The badge shows a bear who is presumably the one who broke the branches. A number of badges represent the geographical feature of the place for which the vessel is named. For HMCS *James Bay* the blue V slices down through the white snowbound land; in HMCS *Kapuskasing* the green forest is the background and the heraldic Y is the meeting of two rivers. Rivers are often represented by blue and white wavy lines. It is worth noting that many originators of the badges have paid their respects to the spectacular geography of Canada.

Unlike other inanimate objects — machines, material and edifices — over the centuries ships have had personality attributed to them. Perhaps this is in recognition of the relationship between men and their ship. She supports them through the cruel and careless seas; unexpected dangers can lead rapidly to disaster but the vessel nurtures the men who nurture her. Personality of the ship implies appellation and while there is no clear documentation of the origins of this custom, one can recall the names *Santa Maria*, HMS *Victory*, *I'm Alone* in the same breath as the names Columbus, Nelson and Joshua Slocum. Over the centuries sources of names have been changed, from Saints and latin phrases, *Dominus Vobiscum* for example, to qualities or inspiring nouns such as *Delight*, *Sunshine*, *Victory*, and *Discovery*, then later, names of eminent persons and finally in the present context of Canadian warships, Canadian placenames.

The official issue of heraldic badges and names is recorded from 1919 when the Royal Navy developed four different *frames* to distinguish classes of vessels. Battleships' badges were in a circular frame, cruisers' in a pentagon, destroyers' and submarines' - a shield, and aircraft carriers' and miscellaneous ships' — a lozenge. For Canadian ships this was amended because names were reassigned to new vessels but not necessarily of the same class. It was recognized to be simpler to retain one form, the circular shape with a rope surround and surmounted by either the naval or the royal crown. Canadian Naval badges are distinctive through their use of three maple leaves at the bottom of the surround.

No account of the early development of Canadian Naval badges can ignore the proliferation of unofficial badges during World War II which were an unexpected product of official policy. At the beginning of the war Canada had only a handful of ships, but over the next five years she developed a navy approaching 500 vessels. Finding names for all these was no small task and for the development of suitable insignias, a committee was struck under the chairmanship of Dr. Gilbert Tucker, the naval historian. One person who also contributed to this committee was "Lt. W.P. Wallace, RCNVR of the directorate of Naval Intelligence, whose knowledge of heraldry made him realize that badge designing was a job for experts. Since no one was available, he did yeoman work himself during the war years, steering the RCN around the numerous heraldic shoals that constantly developed."[2]

Under these extraordinary conditions where the demand for ships outstripped the possibility of keeping up with official badge design, the committee recommended a policy, which was promulgated by the RCN, that commanding officers might devise their own badges. "These were to come under the scrutiny of the Captain *D* or the Captain of the port . . . to see that they contained nothing offensive to propriety or good taste (reference to the enemy excepted)."[3] These, as yet, unofficial badges were often humorous and risqué; they included cartoon characters such as Daisy Mae, Donald Duck, Mickey Mouse, renderings of U-boats half submerged, bulldogs, Winston Churchill and Hitler, among others. They represented the spirit of wartime effort and while they have no place amongst the following badges, they should not be forgotten in the historic bias of officialdom. Only one of these "unofficial" badges was adopted without change and remains in the permanent collection — the badge of HMCS *Algonquin*. Today the Director of Ceremonial, in his capacity as Inspector of the Canadian Forces Colours and Badges, in consultation with the Unit and the Environmental Commander, recommends each to the Governor General, for his/her approval as Commander in Chief. As the badges are not armorial bearings, they are not required to be approved, amended or originated by the Queen's Heralds.

One of the intrinsic elements of the ship's badge is the motto. These slogans, either as battle cries or maxims to live by, depending on their context, are rooted in the basics of specific personal identification. This might be the shout "Hurrah", or more likely a call to the leader, spiritual or temporal. Many are familiar with Henry V's cry —

> *Follow your spirit; and upon this charge*
> *Cry "God for Harry! England! and St. George!"*

The unforgettable motto of revolutionary France was *Liberté, Egalité, Fraternité*. This motto serves to express a mode or aspiration that an heraldic device is unable to convey. So it is with the ship's motto.

As has been said, all Canadian Navy badges are surmounted by either the naval crown, which distinguishes HMC ships from other badges. This ancient symbol is similar to the rostral crown of the Romans. It consists of a circlet bearing the sterns of three ships of the line, each with three poop lanterns and two squared sails spread on a mast and yard, fully fitted and sheeted home. The hulls and sails are placed alternately around the circlet. Its use in England as a badge of naval distinction and honour dates back three centuries, possibly longer.

Just as this regalia is part of the permanent appurtenances of each ship so are the battle honours. They are justly a source of great pride and are prominently displayed in the ship. Since the name outlives the hull itself, so do the battle honours. HMCS *Fortune*, as an example, wears battle honours of the Armada, 1588; Jutland, 1916; Atlantic, 1939; North Sea, 1940; and the Malta Convoys of 1941-1942. The Canadian *Fortune* was built in 1954. The naval historian E.C. Russell wrote:

> Like many of the cherished traditions of the Royal Canadian Navy, shared battle honours is one more symbol of the ties that binds the nations of the Commonwealth as free and equal realms under one sovereign. These and the ancient devices of badge and motto express the sailor's pride in service, pride in wearing the Queen's uniform, and the satisfaction in a task well done.[4]

The following pages illustrate that Canadian Naval badges are as resplendent and diversified as any in the world. To some, one badge alone in this collection will represent their personal source of pride for service rendered, and may refresh, tone and tint, the feelings and emotions which even time cannot subvert. To others it is an introduction to these particular symbols of national heritage and sovereignty.

Lt(N) J. Graeme Arbuckle, CD

1. *Simple Heraldry,* Moncrieffe & Pottinger, Thomas Nelson & Son Limited, 1953.
2. "Symbols and Ships", Beddoe, *The Crowsnest,* 1961.
3. *Ibid.*
4. *Customs and Traditions of the Canadian Armed Forces,* Russell, Edward C., Deneau & Greenberg, 1980.

Badge of the Royal Canadian Navy

Blazon *Within an orle of ten maple leaves gold, an oval cartouche azure fimbriated or thereon a foul anchor of the same, the whole ensigned by a representation of the Royal crown.*

The design of this badge clearly indicates its name: Royal (the crown) Canadian (the maple leaves) Navy (the anchor). Of course, the azure of the oval is navy blue. The badge originally approved on March 31, 1944 contained only nine maple leaves which represented the provinces, but the new design approved on July 17, 1952, contained the tenth maple leaf representing Newfoundland. The final change was made on March 26, 1956 when the Tudor Crown was replaced with the St. Edward's Crown in accordance with the wishes of Her Majesty.

Commander Canadian Fleet

Blazon   *Barry wavy argent and azure a plate charged with a cross of St. George.*

The cross of St. George has been used as a device in battle and command flags at sea since the thirteenth century. In 1545, flags bearing only the cross of St. George were instituted to signify the presence of the various admirals commanding a fleet or a squadron. By 1674 commodores were also granted the use of a *broad pennant* with the cross of St. George as its main device. This practice remains in force today. The field of heraldic water is further indication that the formation is commanded by the individual who holds this title and is authorized to use this badge.

HMC
SHIPS

HMCS *Acadia*

Blazon *Azure, a seme-de-lis or, the head and shoulders of a young woman wearing a cap and shoulder scarf of the period (1755) all in the colour of a cameo stone.*

Set on the background of the old French, and therefore Acadian, emblems, the gold fleur-de-lis on a blue field, is the stylized cameo portrait of an 18th-century woman, who might well be Longfellow's Evangeline.

Acadia was originally a Dominion Hydrographic Survey Vessel which was commissioned into the RCN in January 1917. She was paid off in March 1919, but was recommissioned in October 1939, and finally paid off in November 1945.

Ships Colours Gold and blue

HMCS Algonquin

Blazon *Sable, a base barry wavy argent and azure of four, from which issues an Indian's arm embowed proper wearing arm and wrist bands argent and holding a fish spear in bend argent transfixing an eel or.*

This was one of the best badge designs produced during the war before ship's badges were issued officially. The badge was of such precision in heraldically representing this destroyer's activities in the field of anti-submarine warfare that it has been accepted as the official badge.

There have been two ships named *Algonquin*. The first, pennant number R17, was the ex-RN destroyer HMS *Valentine*, transferred to the RCN in February 1944. She was paid off into reserve in February 1946. After modernization in 1953, she served until finally paid off in April 1970. During this time she wore pennant 224.

Algonquin (II) is a Tribal class destroyer. She was commissioned in November 1973, and wears pennant 283.

Colours Gold and azure blue
Motto A coup sur (With sure stroke)
Battle Honours Norway, 1944; Normandy, 1944; Arctic, 1944-1945.

HMCS *Annapolis*

Blazon Gules, a bend wavy argent charged with a like bendlet azure, and over all a cypher of the letters AR entwined in ornamental script ensigned by an ancient crown, all gold.

This ship derives its name from the Annapolis River in Nova Scotia, which is symbolized by the white and blue wavy diagonal. The letters AR have a triple significance, first for Annapolis Royal in Nova Scotia, for it was after this settlement that the river was named; Annapolis, Maryland, which is the site of the US Naval Academy; and HM Queen Anne, in whose honour these two places were named.

The original *Annapolis* was one of eight four-stacker destroyers turned over to the Canadian Navy as part of the lend/lease agreement between Britain and the United States. She was commissioned in September 1940 and her name changed from USS *Mackenzie* to HMCS *Annapolis*. She was paid off in June 1945.

Annapolis (II) is the lead ship of the Annapolis destroyer class. She was commissioned in December 1964 and wears pennant 265.

Colours Gold and scarlet
Motto To excel
Battle Honours Atlantic, 1941-1943.

6

HMCS Antigonish

Blazon *Argent, a bear rampant sable, langued gules, grasping and breaking with its forepaws a beech bough proper.*

Antigonish is a Micmac word meaning "broken branches." It is said that beech trees grew in abundance at the site of the present town and that bears used to frequent the spot to procure beech nuts from the branches that they broke down, thereby the association with the name and the animal.

Antigonish was a member of the 1943-1944 programme of 27 River class frigates. Commissioned in July 1943, she wore pennant K661. Paid off into reserve in 1946, she was reactivated in 1947, and served as a training ship until 1954. Between 1956 and 1957 she underwent an extensive conversion which greatly improved her fighting capabilities. As a member of the Prestonian class of ocean escort she wore pennant 301. *Antigonish* was paid off in December 1966.

Colours Gold and black
Motto Be worthy
Battle Honours Atlantic, 1944-1945.

HMCS *Assiniboine*

Blazon   *Or, a bend wavy azure charged with two cotises wavy argent, over all a bison's head caboshed proper.*

The unofficial wartime badge of the ship displayed a buffalo, or bison, and three green maple leaves. These unsuitable devices were replaced by the present badge which reflects the wheat fields of Manitoba, and the surviving homeland of the buffalo. Being a River class destroyer, HMCS *Assiniboine* takes the name of this Canadian river, which is to be found in the province of Manitoba.

Originally HMS *Kempenfelt, Assiniboine* (I) was commissioned into the RCN shortly after the outbreak of World War II, and served in ocean escort duty until the appearance of the first corvettes in 1940. *Assiniboine* carried the pennant D18 and later I18 until she was paid off in August 1945. The current *Assiniboine* (II) is a member of the seven ship St. Laurent class. Originally designed as a destroyer escort, the class was extensively refitted between 1964 and 1966, and emerged as helicopter carrying destroyers. *Assiniboine* was commissioned in 1956 and wears pennant 234.

Colours   Black and gold
Motto   Nunquam non paratus (Never unprepared.)
Battle Honours   Atlantic, 1939-1945; Biscay, 1944; English Channel, 1944-1945.

HMCS *Athabaskan*

Blazon *On a field argent, a North American Indian clad in buckskin breeches, leggings and beaded moccasins, but bare to the waist except for a necklace of bear's claws and blue shells, and ear ornaments of the last. The Indian wears the full-feathered headdress and is mounted bareback upon an Indian pony being halted from the trot. The Indian holds a red bow and arrow in the "ready" position, the latter pointing down.*

The badge of HMCS *Athabaskan* is based on that planned by the ship's company of the original *Athabaskan*, but was not finished before the ship was lost in action. The elements of the originally planned badge were retained.

Athabaskan was commissioned in February 1943, and spent most of her wartime career on the eastern side of the Atlantic. On the night of April 29, 1944 she was torpedoed and sunk whilst engaging two German destroyers. She wore pennant G07. *Athabaskan* (II) was one of four Tribal class destroyers built in Halifax between 1945 and 1948. Commissioned in January 1948, she saw action in Korea before paying off in April 1966. She wore pennant R79 and then later 219. The current *Athabaskan* (III), is a member of the four ship Tribal class of DDH's, and wears pennant 282.

Colours White and scarlet   ***Motto*** We fight as one
Battle Honours Arctic, 1943-1944; English Channel, 1944; Korea, 1950-1953.

9

HMCS *Beacon Hill*

Blazon   *Sable, upon a mount vert a cresset or, fired proper.*

The design used in this badge is a rebus on the name Beacon Hill. Commemorating Victoria, British Columbia, *Beacon Hill* was commissioned in 1944, and was constructed as part of the 1942-43 River class frigate programme. She wore pennant K407 until 1946, when she was paid off into reserve. She was reactivated in 1949, and served until 1954 as a training vessel. Between 1953 to 1958 she underwent the refit which produced the Prestonian class of ocean escort. She wore pennant 303 from 1949 until her decommissioning in September 1967.

Colours   Gold and black

Motto   Semper Liber (Always free).

Battle Honours   Atlantic, 1944-1945; English Channel, 1944-1945.

HMCS Beaver

Blazon *Or, four bars wavy light blue, a beaver sejant sable.*

This badge shows a beaver in the posture it usually assumes when at work on a tree, and is used here to suggest that this ship was industrious in all its undertakings, and "worked like a beaver."

Built in 1902 as a private yacht named *Aztec*, the original *Beaver* was commissioned into the RCN as an armed yacht in September 1940. Wearing pennants S10 then Z10 she served until October 1944. The name was perpetuated by a Great Lakes training vessel (ex-ML 106) so named in 1954.

Colours Black and gold

Battle Honours Louisburg, 1758; Athalante, 1804; Heligoland, 1914; Atlantic, 1942.

HMCS Blue Heron

Blazon *Sable, a blue heron in its vigilance proper, standing in a base of heraldic water, barry wavy of six argent and azure.*

In heraldry, the heron and the crane are often depicted standing on one foot, while with the other it holds a stone. The fable from which this symbol originates suggests that should the bird fall asleep, it would drop the stone and awaken itself. This naturally leads to the term — "in its vigilance" — an appropriate symbol for one of HMC ships.

Blue Heron was a member of the Bird class of patrol boat. She was built in Orillia, Ontario and commissioned in May 1956. She wore pennant 782 until she was paid off into reserve in November 1956. After having served as a Reserve and Cadet training vessel, she went on loan to the RCMP from 1957 to 1968, when she was finally paid off.

Colours Blue and white

HMCS Bluethroat

Blazon *Azure, between flanches or, a bezant charged with a Bluethroated bird volant proper, and issuing saltirewise from the bezant four trident heads argent.*

The gold discs are intended to represent mines, or segments of them, as they might be observed at very close range from beneath the surface, in reference to the function of the ship as a minelayer.

The flying bird represents the name of the ship, while the four tridents indicate protection from approaching dangers.

Bluethroat was originally commissioned as a mine and loop layer in 1955. By 1964 however, she had been redesignated as a research vessel.

Colours Gold and blue

HMCS *Bonaventure*

Blazon *On a field barry wavy of ten argent and azure a horseshoe with toe to base or in which a wyvern wings displayed gules gorged with a coronet of Canada.*

This ship's name is famous in the annals of British naval history and retains the original RN badge with one addition, the coronet of Canada as a collar on the wyvern. The name is derived from an island in the Gulf of St. Lawrence which is a bird sanctuary to thousands of nesting sea birds. *Bonaventure* is a carrier which serves as a resting place for aircraft that leave and return to her decks.

The horseshoe in the design is a symbol of *bonne aventure* or good luck. The wyvern, while having no particular heraldic significance of its own, does display the tail of a fish and is winged, illustrating its ability to fly.

Originally HMS *Powerful, Bonaventure* was commissioned into the RCN in January 1957. She wore pennant 22 until she was paid off in July 1970.

Colours Gold and scarlet

Motto Non por nos toz seus (Not for us alone)

Battle Honours Lowestoft, 1665; Four Days Battle, 1666; Orfordness, 1666; Sole Bay, 1672; Schooneveld, 1673; Texel, 1673; Barfleur, 1692; Malta Convoys, 1941.

HMCS Bras d'Or

Blazon   *Azure, issuing from a base barry wavy of four argent and azure, an arm embowed or, the hand grasping a pheon-headed spear in bend sinister pointed to the dexter argent.*

The name *Bras d'Or*, meaning "golden arm" in English, is derived from the salt-water lakes of Cape Breton, Nova Scotia. The badge design depicts the golden arm rising out of the water, the hand grasping a spear armed with a pheon.

The first *Bras d'Or* to serve with the RCN was built in Sorel, Quebec in 1919. As an auxiliary minesweeper, she patrolled the Halifax approaches between 1939 and 1940. On the night of October 18 while shadowing a freighter, she disappeared without a trace.

The second *Bras d'Or* was classified as a Fast Hydrofoil Escort, and with a speed in excess of 60 knots, was nearly ten times faster than her RCN predecessor. *Bras d'Or* (II) was commissioned in July 1968, and wore pennant 400 until being paid off in May 1972. She had been named for the place where the first hydrofoil tests took place in the early years of the twentieth century.

Colours   Gold and blue

HMCS Brockville

Blazon *Argent, a lion passant guardant gules, holding in his dexter paw a fleur-de-lis azure.*

This ship was named for the town of Brockville, Ontario, which was incorporated in 1832 and given its name in honour of the hero of Queenston Heights, General Sir Isaac Brock.

Brock came from Guernsey and his family arms included a blue field bearing with a single gold fleur-de-lis and a lion in red on a white background. The same device on this badge shows one variation — the blue fleur-de-lis in the right paw of the lion.

Brockville was a Bangor class minesweeper constructed between 1940 and 1941. Commissioned in September 1942, she wore pennant J270 until she was decommissioned in August 1943. She was later reactivated and served as a training ship, wearing pennant 178 until she was paid off in October 1958.

Colours Red and white
Battle Honours Atlantic, 1943-1945.

HMCS Buckingham

Blazon *Gules, a swan, wings displayed argent gorged with a coronet of Canada, or.*

The swan, taken from the coat of arms of Buckingham, England, after which the Quebec town was named, is wearing a coronet of Canada instead of a normal ducal coronet. This is made up of a circlet of gold with maple leaves around the rim instead of the strawberry leaves of the ducal coronet.

The red background and the white of the swan refer to the colours of Canada.

HMCS *Buckingham* was a River class frigate, one of the 1943-1944 programme. She was commissioned in November 1944, and wore pennant K685 until she was paid off into reserve in November 1945. She underwent conversion to a Prestonian class ocean escort in 1953-1954, and wore pennant 314 until finally paid off in March 1965.

Colours White and red
Battle Honours Belle Isle, 1761; Atlantic, 1945.

HMCS Cap de la Madeleine

Blazon *Azure, on an Indian tomahawk and woodsman's axe in saltire argent, an annulet on which a shepherd's crook erect or, and over all within the annulet a lozenge argent charged with an anchor azure.*

This ship named in honour of Cap de la Madeleine, a seigniory of the time of Champlain, was founded by the Jesuits as a mission for the Indians. The shepherd's crook is for the pastoral work of the mission and the gold annulet or ring, for the shelter and safety which was provided to the Indians. The tomahawk or "skull cracker", represents the Indians. The woodsman's axe refers to the pulp and paper and lumbering industries of the present day, of which Cap de la Madeleine is a center. The white lozenge refers to the local legend of the bridge of ice said to have been miraculously formed so that stone for the building of a shrine could be obtained from the other side of the St. Lawrence River. The anchor is a symbol of hope and refuge, and is also a reference to the Navy.

HMCS *Cap de la Madeleine* was commissioned in September 1944, and wore pennant K663 until she was decommissioned in November 1945. She was reactivated after her conversion to a Prestonian class ocean escort in December 1954, and wore pennant 317 until finally paid off in May 1965.

Colours Gold and blue ***Battle Honours*** Atlantic, 1945.

HMCS Cape Breton

Blazon *Azure, a spur gear argent charged with a device consisting of three ermine spots conjoined in the center, one pointing to the chief, one to the dexter base and one to the sinister base in trefoil fashion sable, and between them issuing from the center, three thistle blooms coloured proper.*

The spur gear refers to the machinery of the engineering branch, while the ermine is from the arms of Brittany, in reference to the origin of the name, Cape Breton, so called by the fishermen and settlers from Brittany. The thistle refers to the Scottish settlers. There have been two ships of this name. *Cape Breton* (I) was a member of the 1942-1943 River class frigate construction programme. She was commissioned in October 1943 and wore Pennant K350 until paid off in January 1946. *Cape Breton* (II) was originally HMS *Flamborough Head*, and she was transferred to the RCN from the RN in 1952. She was commissioned in January 1953, and wore pennant 100. She was paid off into reserve in February 1964, and is currently used as the Fleet Maintenance Group (Pacific) Headquarters in Esquimalt, British Columbia.

Colours White and black ***Motto*** Le chance ne change pas la course (Chance changes not our course)
Battle Honours Arctic, 1944; Normandy, 1944; Atlantic, 1944-1945.

HMCS *Cape Scott*

Blazon *Argent, a cross azure charged in the center with a thistle or and interlaced with a gear-wheel gules.*

Cape Scott on Vancouver Island was named by Captains Lowrie and Guise in honour of David Scott, a merchant of Bombay who assisted in organizing a trading expedition from that port to Nootka Sound in 1768. These officers commanded the ships *Captain Cook* and *Experiment* respectively.

The blue cross in the badge is taken from the flag of the Trustees of the port of Bombay; the gear wheel refers to one of the functions of HMCS *Cape Scott* as a maintenance vessel, while the thistle is reference to the name *Scott*.

HMCS *Cape Scott* was originally HMS *Beachy Head*, which was transferred to the RCN and commissioned in 1953. She wore pennant 101 until she was paid off into reserve in July 1970. She was reactivated in 1972 as the headquarters for Fleet Maintenance Group (Atlantic), and remained so until 1975. She was finally disposed of in 1978.

Colours White and blue.

HMCS Caribou

Blazon *Azure, a fully attired caribou calling, erased at the shoulder, proper.*

This badge appropriately depicts the animal for which the ship was named. The caribou shown in the design was patterned after the one which appeared on the one cent postage stamp of Newfoundland. The design shows a fine male, well antlered in the pose of calling a challenge to another of the species. The blue background refers to the sea.

HMCS *Caribou* was the former American yacht *Elfreda*. She was commissioned into the RCN in May 1940, and wore pennants S12 and Z25 until she was paid off in July 1945.

Colours White and blue

HMCS Cayuga

Blazon *Or, an Indian of the Cayuga tribe, facing dexter, in kneeling posture, right knee on the ground, left leg bent and forward, two feathers in hair, lower part of body clad, upper bare, a quiver of arrows pendant from the left shoulder, the base resting on ground beside the right knee, the Indian holding a bow and arrow in the "ready" position all gules.*

The Cayugas were always very loyal to the British sovereign, and in times of war fought on the side of the monarch. Hence, the royal colours of gold and scarlet are accorded this badge, and the Indian is shown kneeling with a bow and arrow poised and ready to defend.

HMCS *Cayuga* was a member of the Tribal class of destroyers, commissioned in October 1947. Wearing pennant R04, then 218, she served a total of three tours of Korea, the last in 1954 after the conflict had ended. She was paid off in February 1964.

Colours Gold and scarlet
Motto Onenh owa den dya (Now let us proceed)
Battle Honours Korea, 1950-1952.

HMCS Cedarwood

Blazon *Or, parted in base wavy azure, a cedar tree eradicated, trunk and branches vert, roots of the first in base.*

The badge design shows a cedar tree whose roots are in the sea. The tree is the heraldic version of the great cedars of the West Coast of Canada. This one stands against a golden background indicative of the setting sun in the west.

HMCS *Cedarwood* was originally a survey vessel transferred to the RCN from the Federal Government. Wearing pennant 530, she commissioned in September 1948, and paid off in October 1956.

Colours Green and gold

HMCS *Chaleur*

Blazon *A field pile or and gules above a barry wavy azure and argent, and in the center an equilateral triangle azure bearing a fern leaf or.*

In July, 1534, Jacques Cartier sailed into a deep bay of the Gulf of St. Lawrence. Suffering greatly from the heat Cartier dubbed this body of water *la baye de chaleur* — the bay of heat — subsequently used in naming this ship.

In the badge design, the water of the bay is in the base and the red and gold shafts of the background above it are intended to convey the impression of heat rising, and that it was here that Cartier made contact with the Indians. The fern leaf is a Micmac symbol derived from the legend where Glooscap slays his evil twin brother with such a weapon, suggesting that it is the determination behind the weapon, and not the weapon itself, which gains the victory. The triangle on which the fern is displayed is intended to mean the place where Micmacs live and is shown in the form of a wigwam.

Chaleur (I) was a Bay class minesweeper, commissioned in June 1954. She wore pennant 144 until she was paid off in September 1954. In October 1954, she was transferred to the French Navy. *Chaleur* (II) is also a member of the Bay class of minesweepers. Commissioned in September 1957, she wears pennant 164.

Colours Gold and red

24

HMCS Chaudière

Blazon *Vert, three cotises in bend wavy or, debruised in the center with a plate voided, the inner edge evicted.*

This ship commemorates the Chaudière River which rises in Lake Megantic and discharges into the St. Lawrence almost opposite Quebec City.

A *chaudière* is a large metallic vessel used for warming, cooking, boiling, etc. It is generally agreed that the river received its name because of the effect produced by the spectacular falls near its mouth, which tumbles into a bowl-shaped basin, and resembles a pot full of boiling water. In the badge design, the golden diagonal wavy stripes represent the river while the white circular device in the center has been hollowed out with a scalloped effect on the inner rim to symbolize the basin with its foaming waters.

Chaudière (I) was originally HMS *Hero*, transferred to the RCN in November 1943. Wearing pennant H99, she served until paid off in August 1945.

Chaudière (II) is a member of the Restigouche class of destroyer escort and was commissioned in November 1959. Wearing pennant 235, she was paid off into reserve in May 1974.

Colours Gold and green
Motto La fortune sourit aux braves (Fortune smiles on the brave)
Battle Honours Atlantic, 1944; Normandy, 1944; Biscay, 1944.

HMCS *Chignecto*

Blazon *Gules, a pile azure fimbriated argent charged with a sprig of bulrush or.*

The Encyclopedia of Canada describes the word *chignecto* as being of Micmac Indian origin, meaning "the great marsh district."

The badge design for *Chignecto* depicts the V-shaped device that has been associated with Bay class ships of the Canadian Navy. The bulrush in gold is representative of the vegetation that grows in marshy lands as in Cape Chignecto. The red background refers to the reddish coloured earth of the area, and the narrow white V separating the blue and red areas of the design is an heraldic requirement.

Chignecto (I) was a Bangor class minesweeper. Commissioned in October 1941, she wore pennant J160 until she was paid off in November 1945. *Chignecto* (II) was a Bay class minesweeper. Commissioned in December 1953, she wore pennant 156 until she was paid off in March 1954, shortly before her transfer to the French Navy. *Chignecto* (III), also a Bay class minesweeper was commissioned in August 1957, and wears pennant 163.

Colours Blue and gold

HMCS Columbia

Blazon *Gules, a bend wavy argent charged with two like cotises azure, and over all in the center a dogwood flower proper.*

This ship is named for the Columbia River, one of the largest in North America to flow into the Pacific Ocean. The river is said to have been named by Captain Robert Gray of Boston after the ship *Columbia* in which he sailed into the river's mouth in 1792.

The white and blue diagonal wavy stripes suggests the river, while the red background refers to the fact that its headwaters are found in British Columbia — red being one of the royal colours. The dogwood flower, the floral emblem of British Columbia, highlights the connection with that province.

Columbia (I) was originally the USS *Haraden*, one of the four-stackers transferred to the RCN as part of the lend/lease programme. Arriving in September 1940, she wore pennant D49 then I49 until she was paid off in June 1945. *Columbia* (II) was a member of the Restigouche class of destroyer escorts. Commissioned in November 1959, she wore pennant 260. She was paid off into reserve in February 1974.

Colours White and red
Motto Floreat Columbia ubique (May Columbia flourish everywhere.)
Battle Honours Belgian Coast, 1914-1915; Atlantic, 1940-1944.

HMCS *Comox*

Blazon *Argent, an ox-head erased at the shoulders and facing the dexter sable having upon its head a cock's comb gules.*

Comox is an Indian word, which means plenty or abundance. This rather humorous design of the *Combed Ox* is an innovation in the best traditions of heraldry, including the way in which the ox-head is depicted.

Comox (I) was a Fundy class minesweeper, commissioned in November 1938. She wore pennant J64 until she was paid off in July 1945. *Comox* (II) was one of the Bay class minesweepers, and was commissioned in April 1954. She wore pennant 146 until she was paid off in September 1957. She was then transferred to the Turkish Navy.

Colours White and black
Motto Ut habeas da (Give that you may have.)
Battle Honours Atlantic, 1940-1945.

HMCS *Cordova*

Blazon *Or, a pile barry wavy argent and azure, charged with a lion rampant gules, armed of the field and pierced through the middle by an arrow.*

This ship is named for Cordova Bay, Vancouver Island. Initially, Sub-lieutenant Quimper of the Spanish Navy anchored in Esquimalt harbour, June 30, 1790, and named it *Peurto de Cordoba*, in honour of Don Antonio Maria Bucareli y Cordoba, the 46th Viceroy of Mexico. This was the first recorded visit of any vessel to the port. In 1842 however, officers of the Hudson's Bay Company transferred the name to another port northeast of Victoria which, while named *Cormorant Bay*, was referred to locally as *Cordova Bay*. In 1905, the name was confirmed by the Geographical Board of Canada.

The lion with an arrow through its middle is from the arms of the City of Cordova, Spain. This was placed upon a V-shaped compartment of heraldic water representing the Bay itself.

Cordova was originally the USN motor minesweeper YMS-420. She was purchased by the RCN in December 1951, and commissioned in August 1952. Wearing pennant 158, she served as the Vancouver Reserve Division tender until paid off in April 1957.

Colours Gold and red.

HMCS Cormorant

Blazon *Argent, a cormorant volant, wings elevated proper, in base, three barrulets undy vert.*

The cormorant is a splendid swimmer and is able to travel for long distances under the water. In the air, it is a very powerful flier. These are the qualities reflected in this badge. The base of water has been shown as green (vert), the colour of the sea from *below* the surface, the implication being that both the bird and the ship demonstrate endurance and agility in plying the seas around Canada and the world.

Cormorant (I) was a member of the Bird class of patrol craft. Commissioned in July 1956, she wore pennant 781 until she was paid off in May 1963. *Cormorant* (II) is the former Italian trawler *Aspa Quarto*. She was commissioned in November 1978, and wears pennant 20 while discharging her duties as a deep diving support ship.

Colours Green and white
Battle Honours Quebec, 1759; Minorca, 1798; China, 1856-1859.

HMCS Cougar

Blazon   *Argent, four bars wavy azure, a cougar's head erased or, langued gules.*

The significance of this design is that the cougar or mountain lion is shown in the pose which it would take before a fight. The allusion of this badge being that all and sundry had best take care not to enrage lest they suffer the consequences of a bad mauling.

Cougar was originally the American yacht *Breezin' Thru*, commissioned into the RCN in September 1940. She wore pennant Z15 until she was paid off in November 1945.

Colours   Gold and blue

HMCS Cowichan

Blazon *On a field barry wavy argent and azure, a pale argent on which a chief's ceremonial mask traditional of the "Cowichan" type of the Salish, vert.*

Cowichan is an Indian word meaning "between streams", thus, the vertical stripe in the center of the badge lies between two portions of heraldic water. The mask itself is a duplication of one in the Anthropological Museum , University of British Columbia. It is of the traditional type produced by the Salish, particularly in the Cowichan district of Vancouver Island, and often referred to as the *Cowichan-type* mask. Typical features are the two smaller heads rising above the forehead, and the protruding eyes. Made of wood, and likely painted red black and white, the badge's mask has been depicted as being of one colour, as though carved from jade.

Cowichan (I) was a Bangor class minesweeper, commissioned in July 1941, and she wore pennant J146 until she was paid off in October 1945. *Cowichan* (II) was a Bay class minesweeper, and she wore pennant 147 from her commissioning in December 1953 until she was paid off in March 1954. She was then transferred to the French Navy. *Cowichan* (III) is also a Bay class minesweeper. Commissioned in December 1957, she currently wears pennant 162.

Colours White and green
Battle Honours Atlantic, 1941-1945; Normandy, 1944.

HMCS Crescent

Blazon *Navy blue, a crescent argent defamed with a maple leaf gules for Canada.*

The badge is a modification of that originally used by the RN. The Canadian badge depicts the field as navy blue instead of black, and a single red maple leaf is placed upon the crescent.

Crescent was a 'C' class destroyer. Originally HMS *Crescent*, she was commissioned into the RCN in September 1945. She wore pennant R16, then 226 until she was paid off in April 1970.

Colours White and navy blue
Motto In virtue cresco (I grow in virtue.)
Battle Honours Armada, 1588; Gabbard, 1653; Scheveningen, 1653; Martinique, 1762; "Reunion", 1793; Cape of Good Hope, 1795.

HMCS *Crusader*

Blazon   *Azure, a crusader's shield bearing in the first canton a maple leaf gules for Canada.*

This badge differs little from its original RN counterpart. Only the addition of a red maple leaf in the first canton of the shield belies the change. This cross, the Cross of St. George, was traditionally the emblem that the Crusaders carried when they went to the Holy Land to defeat the Infidels.

Crusader was a 'C' class destroyer. Originally HMS *Crusader*, she was commissioned into the RCN in November 1945. She wore pennant R20, then 228 until she was paid off in January 1960.

Colours   White and red
Motto   By this sign we conquer
Battle Honours   Belgian Coast, 1914-1916; Korea, 1952-1953.

HMCS *Digby*

Blazon *Azure, an ostrich argent, holding in its beak a horseshoe or, and supporting with its dexter foot a bezant.*

The ostrich which is taken from the crest in the arms of William, 5th Baron Digby, father of the Honourable Robert Digby, Rear-admiral of the Red, and Commander-in-chief in North America (1781-1783), in whose honour the town of Digby, Nova Scotia is named. The gold disc symbolizes a mine, in reference to the function of HMCS *Digby* as a minesweeper.

A member of the Bangor class of sweeper, *Digby* was commissioned in July 1942, and wore pennant J267 until she was paid off into reserve in February 1945. She was recommissioned in April 1953 and wore pennant 179 until finally paid off in November 1956.

Colours White and blue
Battle Honours Atlantic, 1942-1944.

HMCS Elk

Blazon *Azure, an elk's head erased argent, ensigned between the attires with a coronet of Canada, or.*

The elk's head is distinguished from the other members of the deer family by the antlers. To indicate that this particular animal is of Canadian origin, a coronet with maple leaves has been placed between the antlers, the heraldic term for which is "attired."

Elk was originally the American yacht *Arcadia*, commissioned into the RCN in September 1940. She wore pennant S05 then Z27 until she was decommissioned in August 1945.

Colours White and blue
Battle Honours China, 1856-1860.

HMCS Fort Erie

Blazon *Argent, out of a mural crown sable, a demi cat rampant guardant gules armed azure, collared and chained or, holding erect a trident azure, the base end resting on the mural crown.*

The word *erie* is of Iroquois origin, translated as cat or panther. In the badge, the demi cat is shown red for its North American Indian origin.

The mural crown has long been associated with forts or fortified towns. Invariably, these towns display in their arms, a mural crown as a reference to this. Fort Erie is no different. Neptune's trident is an effective weapon for heraldic purposes and appropriate for HMC ships.

Fort Erie was a River class frigate of the 1943-1944 building programme. She was commissioned in October 1944 and wore pennant K670 until she was paid off into reserve in November 1945. She entered refit and was converted to a Prestonian class ocean escort between 1953 and 1955. She was recommissioned in April 1956 and wore pennant 312 until finally paid off in March 1965.

Colours   Red and Black

HMCS Fort Frances

Blazon *Azure, a unicorn's head erased argent, armed and crined or, langued gules, gorged with a plain collar of gold on which a plate edged or and charged with a maple leaf gules.*

Fort Frances was named for a fur trading post of the same name on Rainy River in northwestern Ontario. The fort was given its name by Sir George Simpson, governor of the Northern Department of the Hudson's Bay Company in honour of his wife, Lady Frances Ramsay Simpson. As there is no recorded armorial bearings for Lady Frances' branch of the Ramsay family, Clarenceux King of Arms in London approved that the device in the ship's badge should be taken from the arms of another line of the Ramsay family. The device chosen was the unicorn's head, with a collar bearing a Canadian maple leaf.

Fort Frances was an Algerine class minesweeper. She was commissioned in October 1944, and wore pennant J396 until she was paid off in August 1945. She was recommissioned in 1958 as a civilian-manned oceanographic research vessel. She wore pennant 170 until sold in 1974.

Colours White and royal blue
Battle Honours Atlantic, 1945.

HMCS Fortune

Blazon *Barry wavy of ten argent and azure, a roundel sable, edged or, upon which an equilateral triangle or from each side of which a wind argent, the wings counter-clockwise.*

The device used for this badge is taken from Zoroaster's Oracle. Zoroaster is said to have lived around 2000 BC. He was a great teacher and philosopher, and the ancient Persian religion, which was monotheistic in nature, was founded upon his teachings.

Fortune was a Bay class minesweeper. Commissioned in November 1954, she wore pennant 151 until she was paid off in February 1964.

Colours Gold and black
Motto Faveat (May it protect)
Battle Honours Armada, 1588; Portland, 1653; Gabbard, 1653; Orfordness, 1666; Jutland, 1916; Atlantic, 1939; North Sea, 1940; Malta Convoys, 1941-1942.

HMCS Fraser

Blazon *Azure, a buck's head erased or, attired argent, charged on the shoulder with a maple leaf gules.*

This ship is named after the Fraser River in British Columbia, which was discovered by Alexander Mackenzie in 1793, and was subsequently explored to its mouth by Simon Fraser in 1803. The river was named in his honour.

The badge design incorporates the buck's head from the crest in the arms of the Fraser family. Its Canadian association is distinguished by the the red maple leaf.

Fraser (I) was a River class destroyer. Originally HMS *Crescent* she was commissioned into the RCN in February 1937. She wore pennant H48 until she was paid off in June 1940. *Fraser* (II) is a St. Laurent class destroyer commissioned in June 1957. She was paid off for conversion to an Improved St.Laurent class DDH in July 1965. She was recommissioned in October 1966, and wears pennant 233.

Colours Gold and blue
Motto Je suis pret (I am ready)
Battle Honours Atlantic, 1939-1940.

HMCS *Fundy*

Blazon *Gules, a pile azure, fimbriated argent charged with a maple leaf between two fleurs-de-lis, all conjoined on the one stem, or.*

The blue pile refers to the Bay of Fundy, from which this ship receives its name. The red background alludes to the reddish earth of the area around the bay. The white *fimbriation* is an heraldic requirement to mark a division between two colours. The golden fleurs-de-lis pay tribute to the original French settlers. The gold of the device is of course, one of the royal colours.

Fundy (I) was the lead ship of the Fundy class of minesweepers. She was commissioned in September 1938, and wore pennant J88 until she was paid off in July 1945. *Fundy* (II) was a member of the Bay class of minesweepers, and was commissioned on March 19th, 1954. She wore pennant 145 until she was paid off on March 31st, 1954. She was then transferred to the French Navy. *Fundy* (III) is also a member of the Bay class of minesweepers. She was commissioned in November 1956, and wears pennant 159.

Colours   Red and gold
Motto   Verimus altum (We sweep the deep)
Battle Honours   Atlantic, 1939-1945.

HMCS Gaspé

Blazon *On a field barry wavy of ten argent and azure, a pile gules, proceeding from the dexter side, upon which a mullet argent pointing to the dexter chief, with "commas" of the same issuing from the points of the mullet, and between them a fleur-de-lis, or.*

The red triangle symbolizes the Gaspé Peninsula jutting out into the Atlantic. The star and the "commas" are of Basque origin and refer to the claim that Basque fishermen discovered Newfoundland in the fifteenth century and later the Gulf of St. Lawrence, including the Gaspé, long before Jacques Cartier planted a cross there. These Basques came to hunt whales and fish for cod. The fleur-de-lis refers to Cartier and the pioneer French settlers in Gaspesia.

Gaspé (I) was a Fundy class minesweeper. She was commissioned in October 1938, and wore pennant J94 until she was paid off in July 1945. *Gaspé* (II) was a Bay class minesweeper. She was commissioned in December 1953 , and wore pennant 143 until she was paid off in August 1957. She was then transferred to the Turkish Navy.

Colours Red and white
Battle Honours Atlantic, 1939-1945.

HMCS Gatineau

Blazon *Vert, a bend wavy argent charged with two cotises bendlets azure, debruised with a sun in splendour or which is charged with a beaver sable.*

Gatineau receives her name from the river of the same name in Quebec. Nicolas Gatineau (or Gastineau), a notary, civil official and fur trader of Trois Rivières is presumed to have drowned in about 1683 during a fur-trading expeditions down the Rivière du Nord, now the Gatineau. The graphics of the badge are a direct representation of the landscape — river and land. The Sun, the source of life and health, is also depicted in the badge in reference to the fact that annually thousands of city-dwellers trek to the hills, lakes and streams to enjoy some outdoor life. The black beaver is in tribute to Nicolas Gatineau's fur-trading activities.

Gatineau (I) was a River class destroyer. Originally HMS *Express*, she commissioned into the RCN in June 1943. She wore pennant H61 until she was paid off in January 1946. *Gatineau* (II) is a member of the Restigouche class of destroyer escorts. She was commissioned in February 1959. Between 1969 and 1971 she underwent conversion to the Improved Restigouche class configuration, and now wears pennant 236.

Colours Gold and green ***Motto*** In hoc catino potestas (In this ship lies power) ***Battle Honours*** Atlantic, 1943-1944; Normandy, 1944.

HMCS Granby

Blazon   *Gules, a bee's wings extended or, charged on the lower body with two bars azure, and supported between the two front feet in chief a coronet of a marquis of England proper.*

The town of Granby, in Shefford County, Quebec, used the armorial achievement of John Henry Manners, 5th Duke of Rutland, Marquis of Granby, as a civic crest. The town was likely named after the village of Granby, Nottinghamshire, England, but it is also possible that the name was given by George III in honour of the Marquis of Granby, eldest son of the Duke of Rutland. The area was set aside for officers and soldiers who had seen military service during the blockade of Quebec in 1775, and to whom a large number of lands had been granted at the beginning of the 19th century.

The Rutland Arms are remembered in the two blue bars on the body of the bee, whilst the bee itself is a rebus on the word Granby (Grand Bee). The coronet also refers to the Marquis.

Granby was a member of the Bangor class of minesweeper. Commissioned in May 1942, she wore pennant J264 until she was paid off in July 1945. *Granby* was recommissioned in May 1954 as a diving tender and wore pennant 180 until she was paid off in December 1966.

Colours   Blue and gold
Battle Honours   Atlantic, 1942-1945.

HMCS Grilse

Blazon *Azure, the conventionalized outline of a finless fish, argent.*

Grilse is a term which, though of unknown origin, is applied to young salmon on their first return from the sea. Originally a term used in respect of the Atlantic salmon, it is now applied to the Pacific salmon as well. Ounce for ounce, these fish have got more fight than most other freshwater fish. They can be distinguished from salmon by their more forked tail. more slender body, thinner scales and more numerous spots. This badge depicts these qualities in a clean, smooth-flowing design which is quite distinctive from fish forms used in other badges.

Grilse (I) was originally the US yacht *Winchester*. Commissioned in July 1915 as a torpedo boat, she was paid off in December 1918. *Grilse* (II) was originally the submarine, USS *Argonaut*. Commissioned in December 1968, she wore pennant 71 until she paid off in December 1974.

Colours White and blue
Motto Suaviter in modo, fortiter in re (Suavely in manner, strongly in matter)

HMCS *Haida*

Blazon *Or, a base barry wavy azure and argent, a thunderbird of the Haida tribe with wings displayed sable.*

The thunderbird, famous in the legends of the Haida Indians, is believed to cause thunder by flapping it wings. This reference is symbolic of the sound of the thundering guns of *Haida* in action, a sound many Germans were subjected to during World War II.

Haida was a member of the Tribal class of destroyers, and was commissioned in August 1943. She wore pennants G63 then 215 until she was decommissioned in October 1963.

Colours Gold and azure blue
Battle Honours Arctic, 1943-1945; English Channel, 1944; Normandy, 1944; Biscay, 1944; Korea, 1952-1953.

HMCS Halifax

Blazon *A kingfisher proper holding a trident in bend, points upward, or.*

In honour of the city of Halifax, headquarters of Maritime Command, the ship's badge utilizes a principle feature of the city's flag, a kingfisher. The bird is holding the trident of Neptune who was, according to Greek mythology, lord of all the seas. It is symbolic of the Navy's service on the seven seas. The badge is newly created for this ship.

Halifax (I) was a member of the 1940-1941 Revised Flower class corvettes. Commissioned on November 26, 1941 she wore pennant K237 until she was paid off on July 12, 1945. *Halifax* (II) will be the lead ship of the Canadian Patrol Frigate program and will wear pennant 330.

Motto Sior Gaisgeil (Ever brave)
Colours Blue and white

HMCS Huron

Blazon *Or, nicotine bloom gules, seedpod vert, and stamens or.*

At one time the Hurons were known as the Tobacco Indians. This fact is commemorated in the ship's badge which shows the conventionalized representation of the nicotine bloom. This is in keeping with the traditional use of flower and plant forms as fighting emblems such as the roses of York and Lancaster; the thistle of Scotland; the leeks of Wales; the shamrock of Ireland; and our own maple leaf.

Huron (I) was a member of the original Tribal class of destroyers. Commissioned in July 1943, she wore pennants G24 and then 216 until she was paid off in April 1963. *Huron* (II) is a member of the Tribal class of Helicopter carrying destroyers, and wearing pennant 281, was commissioned in December 1972.

Colours Gold and crimson
Motto Ready the brave
Battle Honours Arctic, 1943-1945; English Channel, 1944; Normandy, 1944; Korea, 1951-1953.

HMCS Inch Arran

Blazon   *On a field barry wavy of eighteen pieces argent and azure, a roundel or displaying a saltire gules charged in the center with a lymphad with four oars sable, sail argent, flags or.*

This name was chosen to honour the town of Dalhousie, New Brunswick. At the time a name was to be selected there was a ship of that name in the Royal Indian Navy, and so the town council decided that a suitable alternative should be suggested. East of the town, there was a point of land which jutted out into Chaleur Bay called Bon Ami Point, although it was known to the inhabitants of the area as Inch Arran. Early Scottish settlers had given the point this name, most likely in remembrance of the large island in the Firth of Clyde on the west coast of Scotland.

The badge design shows a round device (suggestive of the island) surrounded by water, upon which is displayed the red saltire from the arms of Bruce, and the lymphad derived from the arms of New Brunswick and from those of the Hamilton Earls of Arran.

Inch Arran was a member of the 1943-1944 River class frigate programme. Commissioned in November 1944, she wore pennant K667 until she was paid off for conversion to a Prestonian class ocean escort. She then wore pennant 308 until finally paid off in June 1965.

Colours   Gold and scarlet

HMCS Iroquois

Blazon *Or, the head of an Iroquois brave, couped at the base of the neck, properly coloured and wearing two eagle feathers in his hair and a gold ring pendant from the ear.*

In 1942 when the ship's company initiated steps to procure a badge the result was the making of an unofficial one in the shape of a shield which bore the head of an Iroquois brave, with his peculiar cox-comb hairdo, a ring in the ear and war paint. The model appeared to be from a painting by C.W. Jeffries. Contrary to proper heraldic procedures, the head was facing the right. When a definite policy regarding ship's badges was decided upon, the head of the Iroquois brave, facing *left*, was used for the ship.

Iroquois (I) was a member of the Tribal class of destroyers. Commissioned in November 1942, she wore pennants G89 and 217 until she was paid off in October 1962. *Iroquois* (II) is the lead ship of the Tribal class of Helicopter carrying destroyers. Commissioned in July 1972, she wears pennant 280.

Colours Gold and black
Motto Relentless in chase
Battle Honours Atlantic, 1943; Arctic, 1943-1945; Biscay, 1943-1944; Norway, 1945; Korea, 1952-1953.

HMCS James Bay

Blazon   *Argent, a pile azure, in the base of which a lymphad with banner of the first, sail unfurled charged with a cross gules and surmounting the mast a sun in splendour or charged with two lines in cross sable.*

James Bay is the arm of Hudson Bay that extends south into the northern part of central Canada. This is denoted by the V-shaped device in blue on the white snowbound land. The heraldic ship refers to Captain James's ship *Mary* in which he sailed from England, which itself is represented by the cross of St. George. The sun with the crossed lines upon it is intended to indicate how the mariner-explorer Thomas James found his was around the seas and coasts of Canada using the sun for navigation. It is thus regarded as a symbol of exploration.

James Bay was a member of the Bay class of minesweepers, and was commissioned in March 1954. Wearing pennant 152, she was paid off in February 1964.

Colours   White and blue
Motto   The true north strong and free

HMCS Jonquière

Blazon *Azure, three chevronels fesswise and interlaced, the central one higher, all proceeding from the base, and within the central one a fouled anchor and above it and touching the peak an annulet all argent within the annulet a fleur-de-lis or.*

This device is modeled on the arms of Jacques-Pierre de Taffanel, Marquis de la Jonquière (1680-1752) in whose honour the town of Jonquière in Quebec is named. The Jonquière Arms display six mountain peaks issuing from the base, and above the central and highest peak a white ring or annulet. In this badge the three chevronels symbolize the mountain peaks; the anchor demonstrates Jonquière's considerable achievements as a naval officer, and the gold fleur-de-lis refers to his position as Governor of New France.

Jonquière was a member of the 1942-1943 River class frigate programme. She was commissioned in May 1944, and wore pennant K318 until she paid off into refit. After her conversion to a Prestonian class ocean escort, she wore pennant 318 until she was finally paid off in June 1958.

Colours White and blue
Motto Au sommet par le devoir (To the summit by duty)
Battle Honours Atlantic, 1944.

HMCS Kapuskasing

Blazon   *Vert, shakefork couped, barry wavy argent and azure.*

Kapuskasing is a northern Ontario town noted for its pulp and power industries. The word itself is said to have originated from an Indian term meaning "branch river" or "divided waters." This is an obvious reference to the confluence of the Kapuskasing and Moose rivers. The badge has a field of green to represent the forested terrain of the area and bears a Y to show the joining of the rivers.

Kapuskasing was an Algerine class minesweeper. She commissioned in August 1944, and wore pennant J326 until she was decommissioned in March 1946. In 1949, she was recommissioned, and served with the Department of Mines under pennant 171 until paid off in 1972.

Colours   White and dark green
Battle Honours   Atlantic, 1944-1945.

HMCS *Kootenay*

Blazon *Argent, three cotises in bend wavy azure, over all a crescent sable debruised by an Indian fish spear-head gules, bound around the hilt with thongs argent.*

The Kootenay Indians were known to have depended for food upon the fish caught in the rivers and on the buffalo found on the slopes of the Rocky Mountains. The buffalo also provided them with skins. The Kootenay River is symbolized by the three blue diagonal wavy stripes. The black crescent is the horns of the buffalo, and the fish spearhead is typical of the kind used by the Indians. It is an interesting symbol for a ship-of-war insofar as the horns and spear can be considered as instruments of either attack or defence.

Kootenay (I) was a River class destroyer. Originally HMS *Decoy*, she was commissioned into the RCN in April 1943. She wore pennant H75 until she was decommissioned October 1945. *Kootenay* (II) is a member of the Restigouche class of destroyer escorts. She was commissioned in March 1959, and wears pennant 158. She has subsequently undergone conversion to an Improved Restigouche class destroyer.

Colours Red and white   ***Motto*** We are as one
Battle Honours Atlantic, 1943-1945; Normandy, 1944; English Channel, 1944; Biscay, 1944.

HMCS La Hulloise

Blazon *Barry wavy, argent and azure upon which a lozenge azure edged or bearing a ducal coronet or through which is enfiled a sprig of three maple leaves vert.*

The city of Hull, situated on the opposite bank of the Ottawa River from the nation's capital, was incorporated in 1875. The name was adopted from the township in which it is located, which in turn received its name from Hull, Yorkshire. In commemorating the town of Hull, the badge for *La Hulloise* shows a "lozenge" which refers to the ship herself, a sprig of three maple leaves in reference to the Province of Quebec and a ducal coronet, reminiscent of Yorkshire.

La Hulloise was a River class frigate. She was commissioned in May 1944, and wore pennant K668 until she was decommissioned in December 1945. After conversion to a Prestonian class ocean escort, she recommissioned in October 1957, and wore pennant 305 until she was paid off in July 1965.

Colours   Gold and royal blue
Motto   Soyons coeur franc (Let us be true of heart)
Battle Honours   Atlantic, 1945; North Sea, 1945.

HMCS *Labrador*

Blazon *Argent, a pale indented azure, upon which an arm erect couped below the elbow or, and supporting with the thumb and fingers an étoile of six points argent, charged with a maple leaf gules.*

The white and blue field with the ragged edges signifies the jagged ice in the water where the ice-breaker has passed to clear the way. The arm is shown in gold because one derivation of Labrador is the French phrase *le bras d'or*, translated as the golden arm.

Commissioned as an Arctic Patrol vessel in July 1954, *Labrador* wore pennant 50 until she was paid off in November 1957. She was subsequently transferred to the Coast Guard.

Colours White and azure blue

HMCS Lanark

Blazon *Barry wavy of ten argent and azure a bull's head caboshed gules, horns proper.*

This ship is named for the town of Perth, Lanark County, Ontario. Since there was a ship named *Perth* in the Royal Australian Navy, it was necessary to find some other suitable name for the Canadian frigate. The town council suggested the use of the county name.

The ship's unofficial badge used a bull's head, and when official badges were instituted, it was felt that this device, representative of the civic crest of Perth and of the fine agricultural lands of Lanark, was appropriate. It is not intended to represent any particular breed, but rather is a stylized heraldic type.

Lanark was a member of the River class of frigates, and was commissioned in July 1944. She wore pennant K669 until she was decommissioned in November 1945. She underwent the Prestonian conversion and was recommissioned in April 1956 and wore pennant 321 until she was paid off in March 1965.

Colours White and red
Battle Honours Atlantic, 1944-1945.

HMCS *Lauzon*

Blazon *Azure, three serpents embowed biting their tails and interlaced or.*

This ship is named for the town of Lauzon in Levis county, Quebec. It is situated on the St. Lawrence River opposite the end of the Island of Orleans. It was first named Pointe de Levy by Champlain in 1625. However, in 1867 when it was established as a village, the present name was adopted in memory of Jean de Lauzon, Governor of New France from 1651 to 1656.

The arms of the family of Lauzon display on a blue field, three golden serpents in circular form, two above and one in base. When shown with the tail in its mouth, it is indicative of eternity. For the badge of *Lauzon*, the three serpents in the family arms have been brought together and interlaced so as to make a single device. The blue background, found in the Lauzon arms, is indicative also of the sea.

Lauzon was a member of the River class of frigates, and was commissioned in August 1944. She wore pennant K671 until she was decommissioned in November 1945. After undergoing conversion to a Prestonian class ocean escort, she was recommissioned in December 1953, and wore pennant 322 until she was paid off in May 1963.

Colours Blue and gold
Battle Honours Atlantic, 1944-1945.

HMCS Llewellyn

Blazon *Azure, a wolf hound sejant and facing the dexter, charged on the shoulder with a maple leaf gules, the dexter fore-paw resting on the ring of foul, wooden-stocked anchor erect, or.*

The ship's badge shows a wolf-hound, suggesting the famous Welsh legend of the Hound of Llewellyn. The right fore-paw on the anchor is an indication of naval association, and the maple leaf is an addition for its allegiance to Canada.

Llewellyn was the lead ship in the Llewellyn class of minesweeper. Commissioned in August 1942, she wore pennant J278 until she was paid off in June 1946. She was later recommissioned in 1949, and served as a tender at Saint John. She wore pennant 141 until she was paid off in October 1951.

Colours White and azure blue
Battle Honours Heligoland, 1914.

HMCS Lloyd George

Blazon *Or, a demi-dragon erased gules, having a chain around the neck and pendant therefrom a portcullis, all or.*

This ship's badge shows the dragon of Wales, with a portcullis hanging from its neck by a chain. The portcullis or castle gate is one of the devices associated with the British Houses of Parliament with which the great Welshman, Earl Lloyd George, was so long connected.

Lloyd George was a member of the Llewellyn class of minesweeper. She was commissioned in August of 1942 and she wore pennant J279 until she was paid off in July 1948.

Colours Red and yellow

HMCS Loon

Blazon *Or, a loon proper, upon a base barry wavy of six azure and or.*

A superb swimmer, capable of the most delicate of manoeuver both above and below the water, the symbol was appropriate for one of HMC ships.

A member of the Bird class of patrol boats, *Loon* was commissioned in November 1955, and wore pennant 780 until she was decommissioned in August 1965.

Colours Black and gold

HMCS Mackenzie

Blazon *Gules, a bend wavy argent upon which a like bendlet azure, and over all a lion rampant or, armed and langued of the third, charged on the shoulder with a hurt upon which a representation of a compass rose of eight points argent, the vertical and horizontal pointers extending beyond the perimeter of the hurt.*

This destroyer commemorates the Mackenzie River, discovered and explored in 1789 by Sir Alexander Mackenzie. A native of Scotland, he was a partner in the famous North West Company of fur traders. The gold lion rampant upon a red field is the reverse colouring of the main device in the royal arms of Scotland. The change was necessary for heraldic purposes, but the device itself is used in reference to Mackenzie and the land of his birth. The compass rose on the lion's shoulder is a symbol of geography, travel and exploration. It is used here to commemorate Mackenzie's great feats in these fields. It is also part of the crest in the Armorial bearings of the Northwest Territories through which the Mackenzie River flows.

Mackenzie is the lead ship of the Mackenzie class of destroyer escorts. Wearing pennant 261, she was commissioned in October 1962.

Colours   Gold and scarlet
Motto   By virtue and valour

HMCS Magnificent

Blazon *Purpure, a sun in splendour or on which a maple leaf gules.*

The elements and colours in this device effectively illustrate magnificence. The regal colours, the glory and power of the sun and the symbols of national allegiance, the maple leaf, combine to form a badge no less 'magnificent' than the vessel herself.

Originally HMS *Magnificent*, she was commissioned into the RCN in April 1948. With her compliment of around 30 aircraft, she wore pennant 21 until she was paid off in June 1957.

Colours Gold and purple
Motto We stand on guard
Battle Honours The Saints, 1782; Dardanelles, 1915.

HMCS *Mallard*

Blazon *Gules, a Mallard duck proper, upon a base of heraldic water argent and azure.*

Like the other members of the class, *Mallard* incorporates the figure of a water fowl into her badge. The members of the duck family are most at home on the water, and their agility in this environment is a suitable characteristic for one of HMC ships to emulate.

Mallard was a member of the Bird class of patrol boat. She was commissioned in July 1956, and wore pennant 783 until she was paid off in September 1965.

Colours White and red
Battle Honours North Sea, 1941-1943.

HMCS Margaree

Blazon   *Azure, three cotises wavy argent, over all a flower of the Marguerite (daisy) proper.*

This ship is named after the Margaree River in Cape Breton. This is a form of the name Marguerite which was the original name, thus the badge depicts the Marguerite daisy on the heraldic illustration of the river.

Margaree (I) was a River class of destroyer. Originally HMS *Diana*, she was commissioned into the RCN in September 1940. She wore pennant H49, and was lost in October 1940. *Margaree* (II) is a member of the St. Laurent class of destroyers. She was commissioned in November 1956, then underwent conversion to the helicopter carrying destroyer configuration. Wearing pennant 229 she was recommissioned in October 1964.

Colours   White and blue
Battle Honours   Atlantic, 1940.

HMCS Micmac

Blazon   *Azure, a fern erect or.*

The Micmac are one of the largest aboriginal groups that was living in the north-eastern part of the continent when European traders first arrived. Their legendary chief, named Glooscap, defeated his evil twin brother in combat with a fern. As a prophet of the Great Spirit, the Micmacs believed that he was responsible for many of the blessings and successes that came their way in peace and in battle, just as he had been successful himself in his struggle with evil.

As a device for the badge of HMCS *Micmac*, the fern symbolizes that although a weapon may be fragile, a just cause may not require might.

Micmac was a member of the post-war Tribal class of destroyers. Commissioned in September 1954, she wore pennants R10, then later 218 until she was paid off in March 1964.

Colours   Gold and royal blue
Motto   Melkedae (Fearless)

HMCS *Minas*

Blazon *Argent, a pile barry wavy or and azure, and over all placed horizontally, a billet gules.*

The Minas basin was so named because of the very rich deposits of copper that were found in the area of the Bay of Fundy. Its exploitation led to the use of the term "the mines" to describe the area. In the design of the badge, the symbol of the basin — the *pile* — is represented in the colour of Royal France. This is in recognition of the early French explorers who preceded the English by one hundred years or more.

Minas was a member of the Bangor class of minesweeper, constructed between 1939 and 1940. She was commissioned in August 1941, and wore pennant J165 until she was paid off in October 1945. Recommissioned in March 1955, she wore pennant 189 until she was again paid off in November 1955.

Colours White and red
Battle Honours Atlantic, 1941-1944; Normandy, 1944.

HMCS *Miramichi*

Blazon *On a field of birch bark proper, a pile barry wavy of ten argent and azure and overall an equilateral triangle, apex to the chief gules, charged with a porcupine or.*

This ship is named for Miramichi Bay in New Brunswick. The background of the badge represents birch bark, used by the Indians in the area for their material needs such as wigwams, canoes and containers. The V-shape is the bay and over all the equilateral triangle symbolizes the wigwam. The porcupine was also important to the Indians, for food and for quills used in both clothing and decorations.

Miramichi (I) was a Bangor class minesweeper of the 1939-1940 construction period. She was commissioned in November 1941, and wore pennant J169 until she was paid off in October 1945. *Miramichi* (II) was a Bay class minesweeper, and commissioned in July 1954, wore pennant 150 until she was paid off in October 1954. She was then transferred to the French Navy. *Miramichi* (III) is also a Bay class minesweeper. She was commissioned in October 1957, and wears pennant 163.

Colours Red and gold
Motto Loyal à la mort (Loyal unto death)

HMCS *Moose*

Blazon *Or, a moose passant sable, on a base barry wavy, azure and argent.*

The badge design depicts a moose standing in water in an attitude of watchfulness. Not only is the animal a strong swimmer, but also has a keen sense of smell and hearing. As such it is very difficult to surprise. It was these qualities that were depicted as attributes of the ship as well.

Originally the American Yacht *Cleopatra*, she was commissioned in September 1940, and wearing pennant Z14, served until paid off in July 1945.

Colours Black and gold

HMCS New Glasgow

Blazon *Argent, on base barry wavy of five azure and argent, the hull of an ancient boat midship on which an oak tree with a red-breast on the tree-top all proper, a signet ring erect or on the forward deck and an ancient hand-bell proper on the after deck.*

This badge is taken from the arms of the city of Glasgow, Scotland. The devices are based on the romantic legends of the life of St. Kentigern, first Bishop of Glasgow who died about 602 AD. The oak tree represents the bough which St. Kentigern kindled by his spoken word into a blaze in order to relight the church lights which enemies had extinguished. On the tree is a robin, the pet of St. Serf which, as legend tells, was restored to life by St. Kentigern. The bell signifies the Church and the Sea of Glasgow. The signet ring is also of legendary derivation being one for which a queen was to lose her life. Yet, the good saint retrieved it in time to save her.

New Glasgow was a River class frigate. Commissioned in December 1943, she wore pennant K320 until she was paid off in November 1945. She was later reactivated, underwent the Prestonian conversion, and recommissioned in January 1954. She wore pennant 315 until she was paid off in January 1967.

Colours White and green
Motto Dum cano cavete (When I sing take heed)
Battle Honours Atlantic, 1944-1945.

HMCS New Liskeard

Blazon *Purpure, a pile argent on which a Lombardy Poplar proper, standing on a stone-strewn and barren mount or.*

This badge is from the crest of the town of New Liskeard in Northern Ontario. The origin of the device is unknown but the tree standing on bare ground suggests something growing on barren ground symbolizing the town's history and ambitions. The civic colours are purple and white, and the *pile* indicates growth.

New Liskeard was an Algerine class minesweeper. Commissioned in November 1944, she wore pennant J397 until she was paid off in April 1946. She was recommissioned in September 1946, and wore pennant 169 until finally paid off in April 1958.

Colours White and purple
Battle Honours Atlantic, 1945.

HMCS *New Waterford*

Blazon *Barry wavy, argent and azure, a dolphin hauriant or.*

This ship is named after the Nova Scotia town of New Waterford which likely received its name from settlers who migrated from Waterford, Ireland. From the arms of the Irish town comes the dolphin of this badge.

New Waterford was a River class frigate. Commissioned in January 1944, she wore pennant K321 until she was paid off in March 1946. After her conversion to a Prestonian class escort, she was recommissioned in January 1958 and wore pennant 304 until finally paid off in December 1966.

Colours Gold and azure blue
Motto Nulli secundis (Second to none)
Battle Honours Atlantic, 1944.

HMCS Niagara

Blazon *Per pale azure and argent, a pale barry wavy of six argent and azure (for Niagara Falls) issuing from which, on the dexter, a demi mullet argent (for the United States) and on the sinister, a demi maple leaf gules (for Canada).*

This design is intended to suggest the peaceful relations that citizens of the United States of America and Canada enjoy, living for many years beside the "thundering falls".

Niagara was originally the American four-stacker USS *Thatcher*. She was commissioned into the RCN in September 1940, and wore pennants D57 then I57 until she was paid off in September 1945.

Colours White and red
Battle Honours Atlantic, 1940-1944.

HMCS *Niobe*

Blazon *Gules, upon two arrows in saltire, argent barbed and flighted or, a lozenge of the second guttee de larmes fourteen in number.*

Niobe, daughter of Tantalus and Dione, was the wife of Amphion of Thebes. Like her father, she had close connections to the gods, especially with Leto, the wife of Zeus. In her maternal pride for her seven sons and seven daughters, she ventured to compare herself with Leto who had but two children. To punish this presumption, the twins Apollo and Artemis slew with their arrows all Niobe's children. For nine days they remained unburied for Zeus had turned all people into stone. On the tenth day the gods buried them, and Niobe, who had been turned to stone on the hills of Sipylus could not, even in this form, forget her sorrow.

Even today, the colossal relief carved on the rocks of Mount Sipylus described by Homer, is washed by a stream in such a manner that it appears to be weeping. Based upon this legend from Greek mythology, the badge of *Niobe* displays on a field of red (for blood), a lozenge upon which are fourteen tear drops symbolic of Niobe's grief. Behind the lozenge are two arrows saltirewise representing the arrows of Apollo and Artemis.

Niobe was commissioned in September 1910, and was paid off in September 1915.

Colours White and red

HMCS Nipigon

Blazon *Gules, in a base a bar fesswise wavy argent charged with a like barrulet azure, out of which leaping, two trout or, one to the dexter chief the other to the sinister chief.*

At the mouth of the Nipigon river is the famous Red Rock on which the Indians painted representations of various objects familiar to them. This is depicted by the red background in the badge. The river is also renowned for its excellent fishing, and to signify this, two golden trout are shown leaping from the river.

Nipigon (I) was a Bangor class minesweeper. She was commissioned in August 1941 and she wore pennant J154 until she was paid off in October 1945. *Nipigon* (II) is a member of the Annapolis class of helicopter carrying destroyer. She was commissioned in May 1964 and wears pennant 266.

Colours Gold and scarlet
Motto We are one
Battle Honours Atlantic, 1940-1945.

HMCS Nootka

Blazon *Azure, in base barry wavy of four argent and azure, a killer whale proper rising from the sea.*

The Nootka tribe were daring whale hunters. They would set out in search of whales after ceremonial preparation, cleansing both the body and the spirit. Considering their small craft, the chase involved much hardship and demanded great courage. If necessary the hunters would jump onto the back of a whale attacking it with knives and spears. The killer whale in the badge is a great hunter, who, like man, knows no natural enemies.

Nootka (I) was a member of the Fundy class of minesweeper. Commissioned in December 1938, she wore pennant J35. She was renamed in 1943, taking the name *Nanoose* and was finally paid off in July 1945.

Nootka (II) was a member of the post-war Tribal class of destroyer. She was commissioned in August 1946, and wore pennants R96 then 213 until she was paid off in February 1964.

Colours White and royal blue
Motto Tikegh mamook solleks (Ready to fight)
Battle Honours Korea, 1951-1952.

HMCS Ojibwa

Blazon *Azure, an escallop shell erect argent irradiated by nine ears of wild rice or, all issuing from two barrulets wavy of the last, in base.*

The design of this badge is derived from an Ojibwa legend in which the migrations of the tribe had been controlled by the rise and fall of the great Megis or sea shell. When the great Megis rose from the depths, it reflected the rays of the sun giving warmth, light and prosperity. When it descended back into the depths it brought hard times, misery and death to the tribe. This was cause to move to a new region in the hope of finding better conditions.

At one time, their migration brought them to Lake Ontario, and the area north of it. Here they found an abundance of wild rice growing around the shores of the lakes. It became a staple food of the tribe, and they credited the great Megis' rising from the waters as the cause of their fortune.

Ojibwa is a member of the Oberon class of submarines. She was commissioned in September 1965, and wears pennant 72.

Colours White and blue
Motto Ne ke che dah (Let us be prepared)

HMCS Okanagan

Blazon *Or, issuing out of a base barry wavy of four azure and argent, a marine monster "Ogopogo" gules, langued of the second.*

This design depicts a fanciful heraldic version of a monster that is said to inhabit Lake Okanagan in British Columbia. Although scientists discount the existence of Ogopogo, the legend persists in folklore and people have claimed to have sighted it. The monster illustrated is purely imaginary, even to being coloured red, when Ogopogo, either real or fable, is said to be of a greenish complexion.

Okanagan is a member of the Oberon class of submarines. She was commissioned in June 1968, and wears pennant 74.

Colours Scarlet and gold
Motto Ex imo mari ad victoriam (From the depths of the sea to victory)

HMCS *Onondaga*

Blazon *Azure, within a representation of the wampum of the Iroquois nation, another of the head of the mace used at the sitting of the first Parliament of Upper Canada in 1792, both proper.*

This design displays a representation of the wampum of the Iroquois nation of which the Onondagas were members and known as the "Keepers of the Wampum." It is referred to as the "Magna Carta" of the League of the Iroquois. Constructed at the foundation of the league, about 1580, it was handed down through a line of hereditary custodians until 1930. The mace head is an indirect reference to the schooner Onondaga, a ship of the Provincial Marine on Lake Ontario. She was involved in the convening of the first Parliament of Upper Canada at Newark in 1792, and also in the founding of York (now Toronto) in 1793.

Onondaga is a member of the Oberon class of submarines. She was commissioned in June 1967, and wears pennant 73.

Colours   White and blue
Motto   Invicta (Unconquered)

HMCS *Ontario*

Blazon   *Or, a trillium argent, barbed vert, seeded or.*

This badge depicts the unofficial floral emblem of the province of Ontario — a white trillium.

Originally HMS *Minotaur*, she was commissioned into the RCN in April 1945 as *Ontario*. She wore pennant 53, and was finally decommissioned in October 1958.

Colours   Green and gold
Motto   Ut incepit fidelis sic permanet (Loyal she has been and remains so)

HMCS Oriole

Blazon *Or, an Oriole proper.*

Surely there could be nothing more appropriate for this badge than the depiction of an oriole in its natural plumage.

Oriole is currently used as a sail training vessel in Esquimalt, British Columbia.

Colours Black and orange
Battle Honours Dunkirk, 1940.

HMCS *Oshawa*

Blazon *Azure, three fish interlaced, or.*

The word *Oshawa* comes from the Seneca Indian tongue and means "the carrying place." It was the site of the beginning of a portage route from Lake Ontario to Lake Skugog. However, Joseph Gould, a pioneer of this district, stated that the word *oshawa* was Indian for Salmon Creek. This it seems, was a term applied to a local stream that well deserved the name. The badge design was suggested by Sir Arthur Cochrane, Clarenceux King-at-arms.

Oshawa was a member of the Algerine class of minesweeper. She was commissioned in July 1944, and wore pennant J330 until she was paid off into reserve in July 1945. She was recommissioned in October 1945, and paid off into reserve in February 1946. She was recommissioned for the last time in April 1956, and wore pennant 174 until paid off in November 1958.

Colours Gold and royal blue
Motto In omnia paratus (Ready for all things)
Battle Honours Atlantic, 1944-1945.

HMCS *Ottawa*

Blazon   *Gules, a bend wavy argent charged with two cotises wavy azure, over all a beaver or, the sinister forepaw resting on a log of silver birch proper.*

This design is taken from the pre-war and wartime unofficial badges of HMCS *Ottawa*. The red background is in reference to the *Outaouas* who were native to the region and the beaver is a device from the unofficial badge of the ship.

Ottawa (I) was a member of the River class of destroyers. Originally HMS *Crusader* she was commissioned into the RCN in June 1938, and wore pennant H60. She was lost in September 1942. *Ottawa* (II) was also a River class destroyer. Originally HMS *Griffin* she was commissioned into the RCN in March 1943, and wore pennant H31 until she was paid off in October 1945. *Ottawa* (III) is a member of the St. Laurent class of destroyers. She was commissioned in October 1955. She later underwent the conversion to the Improved St. Laurent helicopter carrying destroyer configuration, and was recommissioned in October 1964. She wears pennant 229. *Ottawa* (IV) is currently envisaged as one of the new ships being built for the navy. She will wear pennant 341.

Colours   White and red

Battle Honours   Atlantic, 1939-1945; Normandy, 1944; English Channel, 1944; Biscay, 1944.

HMCS *Outremont*

Blazon *Party per chevron or and vert, in chief surmounting the peak of the chevron an ancient crown gules and in base a peacock in his pride, or.*

Outremont, once a village in the County of Hochelaga, Quebec, is now a suburb of Montreal, situated on the other side of Mount Royal from the core of the city. In the badge the green is symbolic of Mount Royal including a royal crown. The gold is suggestive of the lights of Montreal and the peacock represents civic pride in the community.

Outremont was a member of the River class of frigates. She was commissioned in November 1943, and wore pennant K322 until she was paid off in November 1945. She underwent conversion to the Prestonian class of ocean escort, and was recommissioned in September 1955. She wore pennant 310 until she was paid off in June 1965.

Colours Green and gold
Motto Proud to serve
Battle Honours Atlantic, 1944; Arctic, 1944; Normandy, 1944.

HMCS Penetang

Blazon *Azure, an hourglass framed or, with sands argent, the upper cup nearly full.*

The name Penetang is shortened from the Indian word *Penetanguishene* which means a place of white rolling (falling) sands. A great sandy cliff is located on the western side of the harbour at Penetang on the arm of Georgian Bay, and the constant erosion caused by pieces falling away from the cliff is believed to be the reason the town was named this way. The hourglass represents this falling sand. An added reference to the linguistic character of the name is that the upper cup of the glass is full suggesting the derivation from an ancient Indian word meaning "morning land."

Penetang was a River class frigate, one of the 1943-1944 construction program. She was commissioned in October 1944 and wore pennant K676 until she was paid off in November 1945. She later underwent the conversion to a Prestonian class ocean escort, recommissioning in June 1954, and wearing pennant 316 until she was finally paid off in December 1956.

Colours White and blue
Battle Honours Atlantic, 1945.

HMCS *Portage*

Blazon   Vert, in base barry wavy of four argent and azure on which a plough or.

The plough in this badge is derived from the civic crest for Portage la Prairie in Manitoba. The plough represents the ship as she cuts as straight and even path to her destination.

Portage was an Algerine class minesweeper. She was commissioned in October 1943, and wore pennant J331 until she was paid off into reserve in July 1946. She was reactivated several times after 1947, and wore pennant 169 until she was finally paid off in September 1959.

Colours   Gold and emerald green
Battle Honours   Atlantic, 1944-1945.

HMCS Porte Dauphine

Blazon *Gules, a castle embattled argent, masoned sable, over which an escutcheon or bearing a dolphin embowed azure, teeth, forefins and gill gules.*

This ship is one of the Porte class vessels which are named for gates in Canadian fortresses and walled cities. The *Dauphine* gate of Louisburg was the source for this badge. The *Dauphin* was the title held by the eldest son of the King of France, and is also translated as *dolphin*. The spelling here of *Dauphine* is a necessary gender agreement with *Porte*.

Porte Dauphine, pennant 186, was commissioned in December 1952.

Colours Gold and red

HMCS *Porte de la Reine*

Blazon *Azure seme-de-lis or, a castle embattled argent, masoned sable, over which a lozenge argent displaying the eagle of Poland gules.*

Reviewing the map made of Louisburg in 1723, there is no indication that the Bastion de la Reine nor the Porte de la Reine were ever completed. In fact, there was no queen of that name when the term *de la Reine* was applied to these structures. There had been no Queen of France since 1683, when Maria Teresa had died. The next person to assume this title was Marie Leczinska, daughter of the King of Poland, when she married the 15-year-old Louis XV in 1725. For this reason, it is assumed, the heraldic device includes the eagle of Poland. The embattled castle with closed gate is the device common to all Porte vessel badge designs.

Porte de la Reine was commissioned in October 1952, and wears pennant 184.

Colours Red and white

HMCS *Porte Quebec*

Blazon *Sable, a castle embattled argent, masoned sable, over which a third tower with three turrets of the same and upon this tower an escutcheon azure bearing a dove standing argent.*

The *Porte Quebec* is one of the gates of the city of Montreal. However, the badge for the ship of the same name is a derivative of the arms of Montcalm who defended Quebec against General Wolfe. The dove on a blue field, placed on the white tower on a black background, is from Montcalm's arms. The lower portion, — the two towers and gate are common to all Porte class vessels.

Porte Quebec was commissioned in September 1952, and wears pennant 185.

Colours Azure blue and white

HMCS Porte Saint Jean

Blazon *Azure, a castle embattled argent, masoned sable, portcullis or, above which the symbol of St. John the Evangelist — an eagle, wings displayed, inverted, a nimbus around the head and supporting a closed book with the sinister foot, all gold.*

This ship derives its name from the *Porte St. Jean* of Quebec City. It is located on the Rue Saint Jean and was opened in 1667 in honour of the Evangelist. This badge displays the generic gateway for all Porte class vessels. The eagle holds a book representing the Gospels — one of the symbols associated with Saint John the Evangelist.

Porte Saint Jean was commissioned in December 1951, and wears pennant 180.

Colours White and azure blue

HMCS *Porte Saint-Louis*

Blazon *Azure, a castle embattled argent, masoned sable over which a fleur-de-lis or.*

This badge uses the golden fleur-de-lis, a device from the arms of Royal France. The remainder of the badge is consistent with those used by other Porte class vessels.

Porte Saint-Louis was commissioned in August 1952, and wears pennant 183.

Colours Gold and azure blue

HMCS Preserver

Blazon　*Azure, a life preserver argent, cabled or, charged on the center chief point with a maple leaf slipped gules, and within the ring a starburst also argent.*

The life preserver depicted in the ship's badge is a rebus of the ship's name, and the red maple leaf shows its current naval affiliation. The starburst in the center symbolizes the flare that was automatically ignited when the life preserver hit the water.

Preserver (I) was a Fairmile Base Supply Ship. She was commissioned in July 1942 and was paid off in November 1945. *Preserver* (II) is an Operation Support Ship. Commissioned in July 1970, she wears pennant 510.

Colours　White and blue

HMCS Prestonian

Blazon *Gules, four tridents, argent, one pointing to the chief, one to the base, one to the dexter and one to the sinister and over all a roundel barry wavy argent two dexter hands conjoined proper.*

This ship's badge uses one of the devices found in the civic crest of Preston, Ontario. The two right hands clasped in a handshake are shown upon a heraldic fountain or spring as a reference to Preston (Health) Springs for which the town is noted.

An indication of Preston's maritime association is the four tridents pointing in the principal directions from the central device. This suggests that the seas of the world are the home of this ship, and that wherever required, thither she would go.

Prestonian was a River class frigate. Commissioned in September 1944, she wore pennant K662 until she was paid off in November 1945. After completing conversion to the Prestonian class of ocean escort, she recommissioned in August 1953. She wore pennant 307 until she was finally paid off in April 1956.

Colours White and red.

HMCS *Protecteur*

Blazon   *Azure, a silver helmet with five grills or, garnished of the last, and bearing a coronet "fleur-de-lis" also or.*

Through the centuries, the helmet has been considered one of the most important pieces of protective armour a person could wear. Just as improvements in helmets meant better protection for the wearer, the capability to keep any escorting warship fully provisioned and fuelled meant better protection for the ships in her charge. This is the attribute reflected in the badge of HMCS *Protecteur*. The use of the coronet trimmed with fleurs-de-lis, a device of Royal France, lends further historical import to the ship's name.

Protecteur is an Operational Support Vessel. She was commissioned in August 1969, and wears pennant 509.

Colours   Gold and blue

HMCS Provider

Blazon   *Azure, an ancient Greek amphora garnished around the base of the neck with maple leaves, and on the main body of the vessel, a foul anchor erect all of gold.*

The use of the Greek amphora illustrates the earliest use of the earthenware vessels in storing and distributing food and water. Its decoration with the maple leaves of Canada is an illustration of its current naval affiliations. The golden colour of the amphora is used to signify the colour of a major item of *Provider's* replenishment stores, and the blue background of *Navy Blue* shows her current affiliation.

Provider (I) was a Fairmile class patrol boat supply ship. She was commissioned in December 1942, and was paid off in March 1946. *Provider* (II) is an Operational Support ship, and was commissioned in September 1963. She wears pennant 508.

Colours   Golden yellow and navy blue

HMCS Qu'Appelle

Blazon *Azure, a bend wavy argent charged with a like bendlet gules, and over all a fox's mask argent.*

The Qu'Appelle River in Saskatchewan, for which this ship is named, derives its name from Indian legend. The story goes that a man was paddling his canoe down the river when he heard a voice calling. Going ashore to investigate, there was not a trace of anyone but the mysterious incident led the Indians to refer to the river as "Who Calls", in their own tongue, and French explorers later translated it and mapped it as the Qu'Appelle River.

The ship's badge depicts the mask of a fox, attentive to every movement and sound just as the ship uses its sonar (for listening) and radar (for watching).

Qu'Appelle (I) was originally HMS *Foxhound*. She was a River class destroyer, commissioned into the RCN in February 1944. She wore pennant H69 until she was decommissioned in May 1946. *Qu'Appelle* (II) is a member of the Mackenzie class of destroyer escorts. She was commissioned in February 1963 and wears pennant 264.

Colours White and blue
Battle Honours Atlantic, 1944; Normandy, 1944; Biscay, 1944.

HMCS Quebec

Blazon   *Or, a maple leaf vert charged with a fleur-de-lis of the first.*

The badge for this ship utilizes the official devices and colours of the province of Quebec.

Originally the cruiser HMS *Uganda*, she was commissioned into the RCN in October 1944. Renamed *Quebec* in 1952, she wore pennant 66 until paying off in June 1956.

Colours   Green and gold
Motto   Nos canons parleront (Our cannons shall speak)
Battle Honours   Martinique, 1794.

HMCS *Quinte*

Blazon *Vert, a Tudor rose, barbed and seeded or, upon a pentagonal cross pattee the arms being formed by five letters "E" each letter facing and coverging towards the fess point argent.*

The origin of the word *quinte* is not certain. For those who feel that it is a derivative of an Indian word, its meaning still remains unknown. The Latin root of *quintus* meaning fifth gives the rebus in this badge with five E's forming a pentagon, thus generating a cross-pattee with five arms instead of four. The five-petalled Tudor rose is included to stress the connection between the Bay of Quinte and the first settlers who were United Empire Loyalists.

Quinte (I) was a Bangor class minesweeper. She was commissioned in August 1941, and wore pennant J166 until paid off in October 1946. *Quinte* (II) was a Bay class minesweeper. She was commissioned in October 1954 and wore pennant 149 until she was paid off in February 1964.

Colours White and green
Battle Honours Atlantic, 1941-1942.

HMCS Raccoon

Blazon   *Gules, the mask of a Raccoon, proper.*

This badge design depicts the most familiar part of the Raccoon, that is the *mask* or black sections of the face. As well as being part of the overall camouflage scheme of the animal, its dark eyes are almost hidden completely by the surrounding black fur. The cunning, stealth and agility of this animal were the attributes which the badge design wished to convey.

Originally the American yacht *Halonia*, *Raccoon* was commissioned into the RCN in December 1940. She was paid off in September 1942.

Colours   Black and red
Battle Honours   Dardanelles, 1915-1916.

HMCS Rainbow

Blazon   *Argent, a rainbow trout proper issuant from waves of water.*

The rainbow trout was selected for the main device of this badge not only because of the appropriateness of the name but also because this species of freshwater fish is indigenous to Canadian waters.

Rainbow (I) was the first unit to be commissioned into the RCN. One of a class of Protected cruisers, she was commissioned on August 4, 1910 and served on Canada's west coast until she paid off on May 8, 1917. However, she was recommissioned on July 5, 1917, and served as a depot ship until she was paid off on June 1, 1920. *Rainbow* (II) was originally the submarine USS *Argonaut*, and she commissioned into the RCN on December 2, 1968. Wearing pennant 75 she was stationed on Canada's west coast until pay-off on December 31, 1974.

Colours   Blue and white

HMCS Resolute

Blazon *Gules, a pile barry wavy of ten argent and azure, charged with a warrior in tilting armour mounted on a sea-horse sable, trappings gules, and holding with the dexter hand a lance at the rest from which flies a pennant argent bearing a maple leaf gules.*

Named for Resolute Bay in the Canadian Arctic, the badge design incorporates certain heraldic devices found in the badge of HMS *Resolution*. That badge showed a "warrior in tilting armour mounted, lance at the rest, all in gold and placed upon a red field." In this variation, the V-shaped compartment marked with the wavy blue lines represents the bay. The warrior is mounted on a mythical beast found in heraldry, half horse and half fish. The red maple leaf found on the pennant of his lance represents Canada. By placing these on a red field, the ship is entitled to red and white as her ship's colours.

Resolute was a Bay class minesweeper. She was commissioned in September 1954, and wore pennant 154 until she was paid off in February 1964.

Colours Red and white

HMCS *Restigouche*

Blazon *Or, the head of a five-pronged fish-spear erect, azure.*

Restigouche, a river which flows through New Brunswick, is a word derived from the Micmac language, meaning "a river with five tributaries." The fish spear with five prongs is an allusion to these as well as being a contextual weapon of the hunt with aboriginal associations and a graphic reminder of the function of this ship in anti-submarine warfare. The gold background is taken from the arms of New Brunswick.

Restigouche (I) was a River class destroyer. Originally HMS *Comet*, she was commissioned into the RCN in June 1938, and wore the pennant H00 until she was paid off in October 1945.

Restigouche (II) is the lead ship in the Restigouche class of destroyer escorts. She was commissioned in June 1958. After undergoing the conversion to an Improved Restigouche class destroyer escort in 1970-1972, she was recommissioned into the fleet and currently wears pennant 257.

Colours Blue and gold
Motto Rester droit (Steer a straight course)
Battle Honours Atlantic, 1939-1945; North Sea, 1940; Mediterranean, 1943; Normandy, 1944; Biscay, 1944.

HMCS *Revelstoke*

Blazon *Azure, a demi-bull erased rampant argent, charged on the shoulder with a mullet ermine.*

This ship commemorates the town of Revelstoke, British Columbia, so named after Lord Revelstoke, head of the banking firm of Baring Brothers. The badge design incorporates, the bull and the star from the Revelstoke arms.

Revelstoke was a Llewellyn class minesweeper. She was commissioned in July 1944 and wore pennant J373 until she was paid off in November 1945.

Colours White and royal blue

HMCS Rockcliffe

Blazon *Argent, a squirrel sable sejant on a broken tree branch proper, holding between the forepaws a fid or marlin spike or.*

The village of Rockcliffe is situated close to Ottawa. While it has no civic crest, the parklands of the area abound with small animals, especially the black squirrel, and wild flowers are in abundance. The *fid* or marlin spike between the squirrels paws represents the naval aspect of the badge.

Rockcliffe was an Algerine class minesweeper. She was commissioned in September 1944, and wore pennant J355 until she was paid off in July 1945. She was later recommissioned and wore pennant 173 until finally paid off in August 1950.

Colours Gold and black
Battle Honours Atlantic, 1945.

HMCS *Saguenay*

Blazon *Sable, a bend wavy argent charged with two like cotises azure, surmounted by an Indian's head facing sinister and couped at the shoulder proper having a fillet gules about the temples, depending therefrom, tips downward, four feathers of the second pied of the last, and pendant from the ear an annulet silver.*

The badge utilizes several devices from the unofficial badge of *Saguenay* (I) and incorporates several new ones. The black background of the badge is in keeping with what early explorers of the area referred to as the "dark woods" of the region drained by the river. To commemorate the ship's wartime service, the use of the Indian's head was continued. Although the unofficial badge had three green maple leaves, they were not used in the new badge.

Saguenay (I) was a River class destroyer. She wore both pennants D79 and I79 from her commissioning in May 1931 to the paying off in July 1945.

Saguenay (II) is a member of the St. Laurent class of destroyers. Commissioned in December 1956, she was paid off into refit for her conversion to an Improved St. Laurent class of DDH. She recommissioned in May, 1965 and continues to wear pennant 206.

Colours Red and black
Motto A l'erte (Ready to act)
Battle Honours Atlantic, 1939-1942.

HMCS St. Anthony

Blazon   *Sable, seme of Indian arrow heads, points to base and flamant, all proper.*

This ship is named in memory of Father Anthony Daniel, a seventeenth century Jesuit missionary to the Indians in Canada. He was killed whilst defending his mission, Teanaostae, near Hillsdale in Simcoe County, Ontario. On the 4th of July 1648, Father Daniel found himself under attack from the Iroquois Indians while his allies, the Hurons, were absent from the mission. Rather than surrender or try to escape himself, he went to meet the Iroquois and was slain, his body being cast into the burning chapel. He was canonized in recognition of his courage and determination in bringing Christianity to the Indians.

St. Anthony is a Saint class tug, commissioned into the RCN in February 1957. She continues to wear pennant 531, for though no longer in commission, is still active as a fleet auxiliary.

Colours   White and black

HMCS St. Charles

Blazon   *Azure, upon two Indian tomahawks in saltire argent a chevron couped or, above which in the center chief mullet of the second.*

This ship is named in memory of Charles Garnier, a Jesuit missionary to the Huron Indians in the seventeenth century. During one of the Iroquois massacres, he fell a victim to a blow from a tomahawk. He died in 1649. With other Jesuits he had travelled to the new land armed with the strength of his convictions. For his heroic death he was canonized and is now referred to as Saint Charles. The design of this badge depicts the instrument of Garnier's death through the use of the two tomahawks. The golden chevron, silver star, and blue background are from his family arms.

St. Charles is a Saint class tug, commissioned into the RCN in June 1957. Though no longer in commission, she continues to wear pennant 533 as a fleet auxiliary.

Colours   Gold and blue

HMCS *St. Croix*

Blazon *Argent, a cross wavy azure charged with a similar one argent issuing from between the arms of the cross saltirewise four maple leaves, gules.*

This ship's badge makes use of devices which appeared in the unofficial badge of the destroyer used during World War II. A large maple leaf on a shield with a cross laid over it, and three maple leaves which were in common use at the time, have been re-organized as shown; while the wavy bands signify the St. Croix river in New Brunswick.

St. Croix (I) was originally the USS *McCook*, one of the four-stackers transferred to the RCN from the American Navy. She was commissioned into the RCN in September 1940, and she wore pennant I81 until she was lost in action September 20th 1943. In memory of her gallant crew, the devices of her unofficial badge have been transferred to the official badge.

St. Croix (II) was a member of the Restigouche class of destroyer escorts. She was commissioned in October 1958 and wore pennant 256 until she was paid off in November 1974.

Colours Blue and white
Motto Stand, fight, yield not
Battle Honours Atlantic, 1940-1943.

HMCS St. John

Blazon   *Vert, rising out of fire in base proper, a partridge or.*

This ship is named in honour of Father Jean de Brebeuf, a Jesuit missionary who was martyred on the 16th of March 1649 near St. Ignace, Ontario. After all the torture he had been through, his captors were unable to force him to renounce his faith, and to hide their failure, burned him at the stake.

This badge depicts a partridge rising out of a mass of flame, and is intended as a reminder of the legend of the Phoenix, the mythical bird who was consumed by the flames that burned its nest. Even so, an egg survived, and warmed by the sun, hatched to produce the next Phoenix and perpetuate the species. In this same manner, the courage displayed by Father Brebeuf at the end of his life lives on and is an inspiration to all who hear the story.

St. John (I) was a River class frigate. She was commissioned into the RCN in December 1943, and wore pennant K456 until paid off in November 1945. *St. John* (II), the inspiration for this badge, was a Saint class tug, and was commissioned into the RCN in November 1956. Though no longer in commission, she continued to wear pennant 532 until she was paid off in 1972.

Colours   Gold and green

HMCS St. Laurent

Blazon *Bendy wavy of eight or and azure, a white whale embowed, head to dexter base, tail to center chief proper, and charged on the shoulder with a grid gules.*

To design a badge for a ship named after the great St. Lawrence River many references are called upon. First the background of blue and gold, the colours of the French King are derived to represent the flowing river. The White or Arctic Whale is said to be the protective spirit of the river. The red grid is associated with St. Lawrence himself. The day that Cartier first entered the waters of the river coincided with the anniversary of the Saint's martyrdom, supposedly by roasting on a grid.

St. Laurent (I) was originally HMS *Cygnet*. She was commissioned into the RCN in February 1937. A member of the River class of destroyers, she wore pennant H83 until she was paid off in October 1945. *St. Laurent* (II) was the lead ship of the St. Laurent class of destroyer escorts. She was commissioned in October 1955. Later, she underwent conversion to the Improved St. Laurent class of DDH. She wore pennant 205 until she was finally paid off in June 1974.

Colours Blue and gold
Motto Ever on guard
Battle Honours Atlantic, 1939-1945; Normandy, 1944.

HMCS St. Stephen

Blazon   *Azure, a cross, couped, argent, in a sunburst or, and charged with five stones, sable.*

This ship is named for the town of St. Stephen in New Brunswick. The design utilizes the cross to represent the martyrdom of this saint and the rays of glory above it, as well as using the stones to represent the means by which he actually met his death.

St. Stephen was a River class frigate. She was commissioned in July 1944 and wore pennant K454 until she was paid off in January 1946.

Colours   Gold and black
Motto   Faeste befongen (Seized fast)
Battle Honours   Atlantic, 1944-1945.

HMCS *Ste. Therese*

Blazon *Azure, three crescents conjoined, two above fesswise and one below, surmounted by a mullet or.*

The town of Ste. Therese de Blainville in Terrebonne County, about 20 miles from Montreal received its name from Anne-Marie-Therese Duggée, a daughter of Sidrac Sieur de Boisbriand, a brilliant soldier who was granted the fief of Ste.-Therese in 1683.

The devices used on the arms of Celeron de Blainville, who married Anne-Marie-Therese, were a gold, five-pointed star on a blue field, the star being surrounded by three crescents, two above and one below. The design of the ship's badge incorporates these devices into one single device.

Ste. Therese was a River class frigate. Commissioned in May 1944, she wore pennant K366 until she was paid off into reserve in November 1945. After undergoing conversion to a Prestonian class of ocean escort, she was recommissioned in January 1955, and wore pennant 309 until she was paid off in January 1967.

Colours White and blue
Motto En devoir, l'honneur (In duty-honour)
Battle Honours Atlantic, 1945; North Sea, 1945.

HMCS Saskatchewan

Blazon *Vert, a bend wavy argent charged with a like bendlet gules, and over all a garb, or.*

This design reflects the unofficial war-time badge of HMCS *Saskatchewan* which displayed a wheat sheaf or *garb*. This device is taken from the arms of the province — three wheat sheaves on a green field. The wavy red and white stripe signifies the Saskatchewan River.

Saskatchewan (I) was a River class destroyer. Originally HMS *Fortune* she was commissioned into the RCN in May 1943. She wore pennant H70 until she was paid off in January 1946.

Saskatchewan (II) is a member of the Mackenzie class of destroyer escorts. She was commissioned in February 1963 and currently wears pennant 262.

Colours Gold and green
Motto Ready and confident
Battle Honours Atlantic, 1943-1944; Normandy, 1944; Biscay, 1944.

HMCS Sault Ste. Marie

Blazon *Paly wavy of ten argent and azure, upon which a fleur-de-lis ensigned with a celestial crown or.*

The town of Sault Ste. Marie in Ontario is situated on the falls of the St. Mary River. The term *sault* is the old French version of *saut*, translated as "jump" or "leap." The vertical blue and white wavy bars indicate this change in elevation of the river. The fleur-de-lis and the celestial crown are devices associated with Sainte Marie.

Sault Ste. Marie was an Algerine class minesweeper. She was commissioned in June 1943, and wore pennant J334 until she was paid off. She was later recommissioned and wore pennant 176 until she was paid off in October 1958.

Colours Gold and azure blue
Battle Honours Atlantic, 1944-1945.

114

HMCS Sioux

Blazon *Argent, a Sioux Indian head proper facing the dexter and wearing the appropriate feather head-dress of a Sioux Chief.*

The Sioux Indians lived on the western plains of the northern United States and in the prairies of western Canada. The Sioux chiefs were among the first to wear the type of feather headress now so often associated with Indians.

Sioux was originally HMS *Vixen*, and she commissioned into the RCN in February 1944. She wore pennant R64 until she was paid off into reserve shortly after the war. She emerged again, fully modernized, in 1950. She wore pennant 225 until she was finally paid off in October 1963.

Colours White and vermillion
Motto Then I will fight
Battle Honours Normandy, 1944; Arctic, 1944-1945; Atlantic, 1945; Korea, 1950-1952.

HMCS Skeena

Blazon   *Azure, out of a base invected argent, a salmon sinisterwise proper.*

This ship is named for the Skeena River of British Columbia. The word is derived from two Indian words *ikish* meaning "out of" and *shean* or *shyen* meaning "the clouds." As with most of the rivers of BC, the head waters are located far inland among the mountains. Their peaks are often shrouded in clouds hence the literal but nevertheless poetic name. The badge design for this ship heraldically depicts a salmon leaping above these mists. This device is taken from the original, but unofficial, badge of the first *Skeena.*

Skeena (I) was commissioned into the RCN in June 1931. A member of the River class of destroyers, she wore pennants D59 and then I59 until she was lost in a grounding in October 1944. *Skeena* (II) is a member of the St. Laurent class of destroyers. She was commissioned in March 1957. She underwent the conversion to an Improved St. Laurent class DDH, and recommissioned in August 1965. She currently wears pennant 207.

Colours   White and blue
Motto   Go forth
Battle Honours   Atlantic, 1939-1944; Normandy, 1944; Biscay, 1944.

116

HMCS Stettler

Blazon   *Gules, a cross couped argent charged in the center with a wild rose gules, slipped and leaved vert, barbed and seeded proper, and between the four arms of the cross four garbs or.*

The town of Stettler, Alberta was named in honour of its founder Carl Stettler, a native of Berne, Switzerland. The design of the badge incorporates the red field of Switzerland's national flag, in honour of Carl Stettler, and the heraldic wild rose, the floral emblem of the Province of Alberta. The four wheat sheaves, or garbs, reflect the location of the town in the center of an excellent wheat growing district.

Stettler was a River class frigate. She was commissioned in May 1944, and wore pennant K681 until she was paid off in November 1945. She underwent the conversion to a Prestonian class ocean escort, and was recommissioned in February 1954. She then wore pennant 311 until she was paid off in August 1966.

Colours   White and red

HMCS *Sussexvale*

Blazon *Party per fess wavy gules and azure, a martlet or.*

This ship is named for the town of Sussex, New Brunswick. The badge design is based upon devices found in the arms of East and West Sussex, England, each of which displays a golden martlet, in one case on a red field, in the other on blue. This design combines both fields, and the boundary between them is made wavy in reference to the sea.

Sussexvale was a River class frigate. She was commissioned in November 1944, and wore pennant K538 until she was paid off in November 1945. After undergoing conversion to a Prestonian class of ocean escort, she was recommissioned in January 1955. She wore pennant 313 until she was finally paid off in November 1966.

Colours Gold and blue
Motto Non nobis sed omnibus (Not for ourselves alone, but for all)
Battle Honours Atlantic, 1945; English Channel, 1945.

HMCS Swansea

Blazon *Azure, in base barry wavy of four argent and azure out of which a swan with wings displayed argent and holding in its beak or a maple leaf gules.*

The badge design is a rebus on the name Swansea. It shows the swan riding on the sea, holding the red maple leaf of Canada.

Swansea was a River class frigate. She was commissioned into the RCN in October 1943, and she wore pennant K328 until she was decommissioned in November 1945. After undergoing conversion to a Prestonian class ocean escort, she was recommissioned in November 1957. She wore pennant 306 until she was finally paid off in October 1966.

Colours White and royal blue
Motto Floreat Swansea (Let Swansea flourish)
Battle Honours Atlantic, 1943-1944; Normandy, 1944; English Channel, 1944.

HMCS *Terra Nova*

Blazon *Gules, a bend wavy argent charged with two like cotises azure, debruised with a cross of the second charged with a penguin erect proper.*

This ship is named for the Terra Nova River in Newfoundland. This is the first ship of either the RN or the RCN to bear the name, however, another ship named Terra Nova was built in 1884. She was the largest and stoutest of Scottish whalers. It was not until 1903 however that she became famous. She was chartered by Admiralty for service in the Antarctic, and for the next ten years was either associated with or was commanded by explorer Captain Robert Falcon Scott, CVO,DSC,RN. In commemorating his gallant service, the Royal Navy named one of their ships HMS *Scott*, whose badge displays a penguin on a field of heraldic water.

In the Canadian badge design, the white and blue diagonal is for the river, while the white cross on the dark red background is from the arms of Newfoundland. The penguin is in tribute to Captain Scott's abilities, courage and leadership — all in the finest traditions of a naval service.

Terra Nova is a member of the Restigouche class of destroyer escorts. She was commissioned in June 1959, and since then has undergone conversion to the Improved Restigouche configuration. She wears pennant 259.

Colours White and dark red

Motto Tenax propositi (Do not falter)

HMCS Thunder

Blazon   *Gules, a pile vert edged or, charged with a representation of the head of Thor, God of thunderstorms, affrontée, wearing a Nordic open crown composed of a circlet with eight arches all plain and meeting together in a point at the pinnacle, his beard formed into nine radiating coils each tapering to a point with a small spearhead at the end.*

There is evidence to indicate that copper was found and mined in the region of Thunder Bay, Ontario, the area for which this ship is named, hence the red background of this badge. The V section which represents the bay, is in green and gold, the colours as they appear in the arms of the Province of Ontario.

Thunder (I) was a Bangor class minesweeper. She was commissioned in October 1941, and wore pennant J156 until she was paid off in October 1945.
Thunder (II) was a member of the Bay class of minesweepers. She was commissioned in December 1953, and wore pennant 153 until she was paid off in March 1954. She was then transferred to the French Navy.

Thunder (III) is also a member of the Bay class of minesweepers. She was commissioned in October 1957, and wears pennant 161.

Colours   Green and gold
Battle Honours   Martinique, 1762; Havana, 1762; Basque Roads, 1809; Atlantic, 1941-1944; Normandy, 1944; English Channel ,1944-1945.

121

HMCS *Toronto*

Blazon *Azure, a mural crown argent, masoned sable, surmounted by a beaver proper holding in the dexter paw a fid spike or.*

The design of this badge utilizes several of the devices found in the arms of the city of Toronto. The mural crown refers to Fort York, the original fortified town and the beaver represents industry on one hand and the early fur trade on the other. The marlin spike or *fid* in the beaver's paws lends the badge its nautical significance.

Toronto was a River class frigate. She was commissioned in May 1944 and wore pennant K538 until she was decommissioned in November 1945. After undergoing conversion to the Prestonian ocean escort configuration, she was recommissioned in November 1956. She wore pennant 319 until she was paid off in April 1956 and transferred to the Royal Norweigan Navy. *Toronto* (II) will be the third ship in the new series of frigates currently being built. She will have a DDH configuration and will wear pennant 333.

Colours White and blue

HMCS Trinity

Blazon *Gules, an equilateral triangle, apex to the chief argent charged with a pitcher plant proper, and having on each side of the triangle arranged counter clockwise, a lion passant guardant or, langued gules.*

This ship takes her name from Trinity Bay which lies to the northwest of the Avalon Peninsula in Newfoundland. It is widely believed that the Channel Islanders were among the first to occupy Newfoundland, and the regularity with which names of bays and inhabited places in Newfoundland match names in the Channel Islands lends credibility to this opinion. With this fact in mind, the badge design makes use of a device from the arms of the Channel Islands, which is also found in the arms of England — the three lions here arranged in a triangle instead of one above the other. The triangle is of course the concept of the trinity, within which is the provincial flower of Newfoundland, the pitcher plant.

Trinity was a Bay class minesweeper. She was commissioned into the RCN in July 1953 and wore pennant 157 until she was paid off in June 1954.

Colours Gold and red

HMCS Ungava

Blazon   *Parted in fess azure and argent, in the fess honour point a roundel of the first surrounded sable, in the base of which barry wavy of six argent and azure from which issues a demi polar bear proper.*

Ungava Bay is found in the northeast coast of Quebec. It is a word of Eskimo origin, and it is generally considered that it means far away or unknown far away land. This ingenious badge suggests a spy glass view of a polar bear, the mightiest of mammals that inhabits this remote region. Its attributes as a predator and swimmer hold it in good stead as a symbol for a warship.

Ungava (I) was a Bangor class minesweeper. Commissioned in September 1941, she wore pennant J149 until she was paid off in October 1945. *Ungava* (II) was a Bay class minesweeper. She was commissioned in June 1954 and wore pennant 148 until she was paid off in August 1957.

Colours   White and blue
Battle Honours   Atlantic, 1941-1945.

HMCS *Victoriaville*

Blazon *Argent, a saltire gules upon the center of which an oak tree charged with a royal coronet all proper.*

The town of Victoriaville, in Quebec, is located in an area formerly referred to as the *bois francs* region. It was heavily forested with the hardwood varieties such as oak, elm, birch and so on. The badge design includes this reference and the Royal coronet for Queen Victoria. The red saltire is from the civic arms of Victoriaville.

Victoriaville was a River class frigate. She was commissioned in November 1944 and wore pennant K684 until she was paid off in November 1945. She later underwent conversion to the Prestonian ocean escort configuration, and recommissioned in September 1959. She wore pennant 320 until finally paid off in December 1973.

Colours Gold and green
Motto Domine dirige nos (Direct us, O Lord)
Battle Honours Atlantic, 1945.

HMCS Wallaceburg

Blazon *Gules, a demi lion erased argent with a chaplet of oak and maple leaves or.*

This ship is named for the town of Wallaceburg, Ontario. The ship's badge uses heraldic devices found in the civic crest. The chaplet takes a branch of maple and one of oak to encircle the lion on the red background. This is derived from the arms of Sir William Wallace, the great champion of Scottish independence.

Wallaceburg, an Algerine class minesweeper was commissioned into the RCN in November 1943. She wore pennant J336 until she was paid off into reserve in October 1946. Later recommissioned, she wore pennant 172 until she was finally paid off in September 1957.

Colours White and scarlet
Battle Honours Atlantic, 1944-1945.

HMCS *Warrior*

Blazon *Azure, the head and shoulders of a Viking proper wearing the typical Viking helmet argent, wings or, coat of mail argent trimmed or.*

This ship commemorates the ability, skill and daring of the earliest sailors of the Atlantic — the Vikings. In little more than a large canoe they were able to withstand the most distasteful of weather and were known to have crossed the Atlantic Ocean to Newfoundland 500 years before Columbus. In addition the Vikings were feared for their ferocity as warriors — in early days "viking" and "warrior" were synonymous.

Warrior was originally HMS *Warrior*. She was commissioned into the RCN in January 1946, and with her compliment of 30 aircraft, she wore pennant 31 until she was paid off in March 1948.

Colours Gold and blue
Motto Haul together
Battle Honours The Saints, 1782; Copenhagen, 1801; Jutland; 1916.

HMCS Whitethroat

Blazon *Argent, between the flanches gules, a torteau charged with a Whitethroat bird volant proper, and issuing saltirewise from the torteau four trident heads sable.*

This badge design utilizes much the same design as *Bluethroat*'s badge does in depicting the mines that this ship was called upon to lay. The tridents are used to indicate that minefields can give all-round protection from attack.

Whitethroat was commissioned into the RCN in December 1944. She was paid off to become a civilian-manned auxiliary vessel (CNAV) in May 1946. Recommissioned for a short time, between April 1951 and September 1954, she wore pennant 113.

Colours Red and White
Battle Honours Atlantic, 1945.

HMCS Winnipeg

Blazon   *Azure, a bison head passant, or.*

This ship is named for the city of Winnipeg, Manitoba, and as such, utilizes certain of the devices found in the civic arms. These arms are composed of a crest above a shield. The shield displays three wheat sheaves over which is a locomotive engine, while the crest incorporates a buffalo. The arms themselves were adopted by the council of Winnipeg on June 1, 1784.

Winnipeg was an Algerine class minesweeper. She was commissioned in July 1943 and wore pennant J337 until she was paid off into reserve in January 1946. She was recommissioned in 1956 and wore pennant until finally paid off in August 1959, at which time she was transferred to the Belgian Navy. *Winnipeg* (II) will be one of the new series of frigates and will wear pennant 338.

Colours   Gold and azure blue
Battle Honours   Atlantic, 1943-1945.

HMCS Wolf

Blazon *Argent, a wolf's head erased sable, langued gules.*

This badge design shows a ferocious wolf's head as its main device in reference to this animal's ability to single out a potential target, track it and regardless of the time involved, make a kill.

Originally the American yacht *Blue Water*, she was commissioned into the RCN as an armed yacht in October 1940. She wore pennant Z16 until she was paid off in May 1945.

Colours Black and white
Battle Honours Barfleur, 1692.

HMCS Yukon

Blazon   *Gules, a bend wavy or charged with a like bendlet azure, and over all a Malamute sled dog, proper.*

This badge uses the Malamute sled dog from the arms of the Yukon Territory. The wavy diagonal of blue and gold refers to the Yukon River along which gold deposits have been found.

Yukon is a member of the Mackenzie class of destroyer escorts. She was commissioned in May 1963 and wears pennant 263.

Colours   White and red
Motto   Only the fit survive

RESERVE
DIVISIONS

HMCS Brunswicker

Blazon *Or, upon a base barry wavy of four vert and or, a lymphad or ancient galley with oars in action sable, mainsail gules upon which is displayed the "White horse of Brunswick" and from the main a pennant gules, and from the fore and mizzen a flag gules bearing a maple leaf or.*

This reserve division is located in Saint John, New Brunswick. It utilizes several of the heraldic devices to be found in the arms of the province of New Brunswick. The white horse on the mainsail is the dominating device which is intended to suggest the name *Brunswicker*.

Brunswicker commemorates a provincial government vessel which served against American privateers in the War of 1812. Another name was considered for the division, HMCS *Dart*, after a privateer that came to be known in the war of 1812.

Colours Gold and black

HMCS Cabot

Blazon   *Argent a Maltese cross gules charged with a fouled anchor or.*

Inscribed on the world map of 1544, now called the Paris Map, is a brief description of the discovery of the *Land First Seen* by John Cabot and his son Sebastian on the morning of June 24, 1497. To a large island which was near this land they gave the name St. John, in honour of the day — the feast of St. John the Baptist. This later became Belle Isle and has remained so to this day. The Naval division of HMCS *Cabot* is situated in St. John's, Newfoundland. The Maltese cross of the Knights of Saint John is the heraldic representation of these facts. Its red colour is the Canadian touch. The foul anchor signifies it is a naval division.

This division was established on September 20, 1949.

Colours   White and vermillion

HMCS Carleton

Blazon *On a field barry wavy of eight argent and azure, the crest from the arms of Sir Guy Carleton, Baron Dorchester, which is "A dexter arm embowed and naked to the elbow, the shirt sleeve folded above the elbow argent, and vested gules; the hand grasping an arrow in bend sinister, point downwards" proper.*

This division, located in Ottawa, is named after the British Schooner HMS *Carleton*, which took part in the Battle of Vancouver Island on October 11, 1776. There is ample evidence that this ship herself was named in honour of Sir Guy Carleton, the individual credited with having saved Canada for the British through the defeat of Montgomery and Arnold at Quebec, New Year's Eve, 1775-1776.

In the badge design, the Carleton arms is place on the field of heraldic water. This symbol of form clearly shows that service to crown and country has been made on land and at sea.

This division was established on November 1, 1941, and remained active till May 22, 1942. Between this time and her reactivation on November 23, 1942, it is believed that the site became the WRCNS training establishment.

Colours   White and scarlet
Motto   Vincemus armis (With these arms we shall conquer)
Battle Honours   Lake Champlain, 1776.

136

HMCS Cataraqui

Blazon   *Azure, a patte de griffon or.*

The badge design incorporates a device taken from the arms of Count Frontenac, which bore three such griffin's feet upon a blue field.

In 1673, Frontenac met and established friendly relations with the Iroquois Indians at Cataraqui and later established the first fort and stores there. The fur traders, finding themselves in need of ships to carry their goods, sponsored the construction of four ships at the port. One completed in 1678 was aptly named Cataraqui. This marked the inception of ship building in the area, and although the Indian village was later renamed by the French Fort Frontenac, and then later by the British to Kingston, the affinity to ships and the sea remains.

Kingston has a rich naval history. It served as the base of operations for the fleet in the war of 1812, and a great deal of activity centered around HM Dockyard there. Everything that this area was, and all that it has become can be traced back to Frontenac who established the settlement, and there can be no more appropriate badge to show this than one which incorporates a device from his coat of arms.

This division was established on November 1, 1941.

Colours   Gold and azure blue
Motto   Porta lacuum, portus classis (Gate of the lakes, port of the fleet)

HMCS Chatham

Blazon *Azure, a stork proper, beaked and armed or, its dexter foot resting on a fouled anchor argent, cabled or.*

This badge design incorporates a device from the crest of arms of Sir John Pitt, Second Earl of Chatham, who was First Lord of the Admiralty from 1788 to 1794. It was during this period that Captain George Vancouver was conducting his explorations of the west coast of Canada, and had a ship named *Chatham* in company.

Originally established for the NOIC in Prince Rupert in June 1940, this division was commissioned on April 1, 1942 and served until some time in 1945. *Chatham* became a reserve division on October 21, 1946 and decommissioned on March 31, 1964.

Colours Gold and azure blue
Battle Honours Quiberon Bay, 1759; Dardanelles, 1915-1916.

HMCS *Chippawa*

Blazon *Azure, an anchor upon two tomahawks in saltire argent, and over all at the fess-point a garb or.*

This division commemorates HMS *Chippawa* one of the ships of Commander Robert H. Barclay on Lake Erie in 1812-1813.

The design incorporates the blue background to represent the sea, the tomahawks or "skull crackers" in reference to the Chippawa Tribe of Indians, the wheat sheaf as an indication of the location of the division, and the anchor to represent the naval affiliation.

This division was established in Winnipeg on November 1, 1941.

Colours White and azure blue.

HMCS *Discovery*

Blazon   *Azure, a shake-fork argent supporting in the middle chief a bezant.*

This badge design does not incorporate any devices which have historical reference to the name *Discovery*. Instead, an ancient form of heraldry has been used which is best described by the French expression *armes parlantes* or speaking arms. Through this form of heraldry, the badge depicts various items which illustrate the different syllables of the name. The design then — *DISC OVER Y*, is a neat rebus on the name of this division.

The design of this badge was suggested by the late Sir Arthur W. Cochrane, KCVO, Clarenceux King of Arms, and through its heraldic interpretation, has become one of the most unusual badges in the Canadian collection.

This division was established in Vancouver on November 1, 1941.

Colours   White and blue
Battle Honours   Portland, 1653; Copenhagen, 1801.

HMCS Donnacona

Blazon *Argent, three maple leaves conjoined on the one stem gules, and in base of the stem, an Indian's dexter hand and a white man's dexter hand clasped together proper.*

This badge represents the meeting of European explorers and aboriginal inhabitants in the personalities of Jacques Cartier and Donnacona in 1534. The three maple leaves on one stem could signify the three nations as one, English, Indian and French.

This division was established in Montreal on October 26, 1943.

Colours Black and vermillion

HMCS Griffon

Blazon *Argent, a griffin segreant azure, seme-de-lis or, beaked and fore-legged gules.*

The badge of this division incorporates the device which clearly represents her name, the mythical griffin. Since the name is taken from a French ship which was built by La Salle in 1679, and used on the upper Great Lakes, the name is written in French, and is depicted with the colours and devices of Royal France.

This division was established in Thunder Bay Ontario on November 1, 1941.

Colours White and royal blue

HMCS Hunter

Blazon *Vert, a crossbow or in bend sinister with two arrows argent interlaced, one on either side of the crossbow shaft.*

This badge design has been inherited from the Royal Navy . The original design showed the two arrows stopping short of the cord on the bow, whereas the Canadian design shows the arrows extended and interlaced with the bow, making it a single device as opposed to three.

In the early days of fighting ships, before the advent of the *great gun*, cross- and long-bows were the principle armament. They had a great effect, for not only were they deadly at close range (the cross-bow was designed to penetrate armour and mail), but when all the archers fired at the same time, it was very disconcerting for the opposition to see a wall of arrows.

This division was established in Windsor, Ontario on November 1, 1941.

Colours Gold and hunter green
Battle Honours Gabbard, 1653; Scheveningen, 1653; Barfleur, 1692; Vigo, 1702; Velez Malaga, 1704; Louisburg, 1758; Quebec, 1759; Atlantic, 1939-1944; Narvik, 1940; Salerno, 1943; South France, 1944; Agean, 1944; Burma, 1945.

HMCS Malahat

Blazon *Per chevron azure and vert, in chief a demi-sun or, rising from the base.*

This badge incorporates devices which tell of the division's location and surroundings. The green sector is intended to represent mountains, most especially the Malahat range on Vancouver Island. The sun can also be found in the arms of the province of British Columbia. The blue is representative of the waters surrounding the division, located in Esquimalt, British Columbia.

Originally the recruiting center in Victoria, British Columbia from January 1944 to January 1946, the division was established on April 23, 1947.

Colours Gold and dark green
Motto Navis exercitatione parata (A ship prepared by training)

HMCS Montcalm

Blazon   *Party per pale gules and azure, a tower with three turrets argent, masoned sable.*

This badge incorporates not only devices to show the French and English history of Quebec, but also to pay tribute to one hero from the early struggle between the two founding nations.

In the second and third quarters of the arms of General Marquis de Montcalm is found: *Sable, a tower with three turrets, argent.*

This tower is now shown on a field equally divided red and blue, the references to the English and French.

This division was established in Quebec City on November 1, 1941.

Colours   Black and scarlet

HMCS *Nonsuch*

Blazon   *Or, a beaver rampant proper, gorged with a collar gules edged or, upon which a roundel displaying the device of St. George.*

This division derives its name from the ketch that brought the early merchant adventurers to Hudson's Bay in 1668. Two years later, the Hudson's Bay Company received its charter, and a trading post and fort were established at what is now Edmonton. So widespread were the activities of the company, that there is little doubt that the organization played a major role in ensuring that this area remained firmly under British jurisdiction.

The arms of the Hudson's Bay Company are basically the Cross of St. George, with a beaver (in black) displayed in each quarter. This badge makes an amusing heraldic joke of a lion rampant proper by showing a beaver with tongue out, standing erect. The gold background refers to wealth of oil and wheat in the area of Edmonton.

This division was established in Edmonton on November 1, 1941.

Colours   Gold and scarlet
Motto   A campis ad maria (From the prairies to the sea)
Battle Honours   Kentish Knock, 1652; Portland, 1653; Gabbard, 1653; Texel, 1673; St Lucia, 1778; The Saints, 1782; Jutland, 1916.

HMCS Patriot

Blazon *Argent, within an annulet of chain links joined together twenty-two in number, a maple leaf gules on which a cartouche or, charged with a fouled anchor sable.*

This circle of links joined together symbolizes the past and present Naval Reserve Divisions of Canada. The maple leaf with oval and anchor is a device used on the unofficial badge of one of the first destroyers in the Canadian Navy, HMCS *Patriot*. The whole design is intended to suggest that Canada's Reserve Divisions form a strong and unbroken part of the country's naval heritage. One only has to review the history of armed conflict to see that RCNR and RCNVR figure prominently in the lists of those who served crown and country. This is the tradition that persists today amongst the Reservists across Canada, and as they are proud of their heritage, so is their country proud of them. The annulet, or ring of chain, is used here to represent all the divisions grouped together as one unit, and any subsequent increase or decrease in the number of divisions will not alter the symbolism of the device.

The establishment in Hamilton Ontario was used by the Commanding Officer, Naval Divisions from February 1,1956 until 1966.

Colours   Blue and white

147

HMCS *Prevost*

Blazon *Argent, a demi-lion rampant azure, charged upon the shoulder with a mural crown or, the sinister paw grasping a sword erect proper, pommel and hilt or.*

This ship is named after the *Lady Prevost* a ship which was actively engaged in the Battle of Lake Erie in 1813. The badge design incorporates devices from the arms of Sir George Prevost, who was the Governor of Canada in 1811, and Commander-in-chief of the British forces in Canada during the war of 1812. It was during his tenure in this post that the Battle of Lake Erie was fought.

This division was established in London, Ontario on November 1, 1941, and remained active until November 30, 1964.

Colours White and azure blue

HMCS Quadra

Blazon *Or, three bends gules, a tower embattled argent, masoned sable, port and window azure.*

This Sea Cadet Training Establishment is named after the Spanish Naval Captain and Navigator, Juan Francisco de la Bodega y Quadra. In addition to a distinguished naval career, he made two voyages to the northwest coast of America. In 1792, he was sent to Nootka Sound on Vancouver Island as Spanish envoy to arrange with Captain George Vancouver for the restoration of British properties seized by the Spaniards in 1789. The two men became friends, and out of respect, Vancouver named the island "The Island of Quadra and Vancouver," and so it appeared on charts of that time. The badge for *Quadra* is a composite of the principle elements of the Quadra arms.

This establishment re-commissions each summer, and was first established on January 1, 1956. It is located at Comox, British Columbia.

Colours Red and gold

149

HMCS Queen

Blazon *Or, a lozenge purpure charged with an orb of the first.*

The last of a long line of HM ships to be named *Queen* departed Halifax, Nova Scotia, on October 18, 1946. She was an escort carrier and had been part of the lend/lease agreement between Britain and the United States, and she was now being returned to Norfolk, Virginia. The day before she sailed, her commanding officer presented the ship's badge to the Regina division, HMCS *Queen*.

The badge design incorporates the devices one would usually associate with such a name. Purple and gold are royal colours, the *lozenge* is a heraldic symbol used in the arms of distinguished women, and the orb a symbol of regal authority.

The division was first established in Regina, Saskatchewan on November 1, 1941, and decommissioned in November 1964. She recommissioned on September 28, 1975.

Colours Purple and gold
Motto Augusta invictaque (Majestic and Invincible)
Battle Honours Ushant, 1781; "First Of June" 1794; Groix Island, 1795; Crimea, 1854-1855; Dardanelles, 1915; Atlantic, 1944; Norway, 1945; Arctic, 1945.

HMCS Queen Charlotte

Blazon   *On a field barry wavy of ten argent and azure, a bull's head sable, armed argent and crowned with a ducal coronet gules; pendant from the nostrils an annulet argent.*

This division is named for the corvette which was built in Amherstburg in 1809 and served in the Provincial Marine on Lake Erie. It had been named in honour of Queen Charlotte, wife of King George III. She was the daughter of Charles Louis, Duke of Mechlinburg, and for this reason the bull's head from the family arms, with slight modification, has been chosen as the ship's badge.

This division was established in Charlottetown, Prince Edward Island on November 1, 1941 and decommissioned on December 15, 1964.

Colours   Black and red

Battle Honours   "First Of June" 1794; Groix Island, 1795; Algiers, 1816.

HMCS *Scotian*

Blazon   *Argent, on a saltire couped argent, a roundel barry wavy of nine argent and azure, charged with a maple leaf gules.*

This division's badge uses the cross of St. Andrew as it appears in the provincial flag of Nova Scotia. Because *Scotian* is part of a larger, Canada-wide organization of sailors, the saltire is marked in the center with a roundel bearing the red maple leaf, emblem of Canada.

Originally *Scotian* was the establishment for the Commodore Superintendent of Halifax and the east coast from June 1944 until late 1945. The division was established in Halifax on April 23, 1947.

Colours   White and azure blue

HMCS Star

Blazon *Azure, an estoile (star) or charged with a maple leaf gules.*

This division commemorates one of the vessels used on Lake Ontario during the war of 1812. The continuing Canadian affiliation is illustrated through the use of the heraldic red maple leaf. The division was established on November 1, 1941 in Hamilton, Ontario.

Colours Gold and royal blue
Battle Honours Dover, 1652; Martinique, 1809; Guadeloupe, 1810.

HMCS *Tecumseh*

Blazon   *Sable, an annulet argent, debruised with a panther crouching to spring or.*

The name Tecumseh is said to mean a panther crouching to spring, or a meteor, which was called by the Indians the panther of the sky. Apparently when Tecumseh was approaching manhood, he went off into the forest alone to endure hardship and fasting, in order to prove himself worthy of becoming a brave. After days of hunger and roaming in the deep forests he lay down exhausted beside a brook where he fell asleep. He dreamed there was a cluster of stars out of which shot one that was brighter than the rest, and which had a long tail. This flaming meteor, which resembled a crouching panther ready to spring, recurred a number of times so that Tecumseh accepted this as his symbol, and the radiant guardian of his destiny.

In recognition of Tecumseh's bravery and leadership in uniting the various tribes from the south Mississippi to Canada to form a confederacy, the annulet or circle is introduced into the design to suggest the unity which he achieved.

This division was established in Calgary Alberta on November 1, 1941.

Colours   Gold and black

HMCS Unicorn

Blazon *Azure, a winged unicorn rampant argent, armed, unguled crined and winged or.*

This badge design was furnished by Admiralty who have graciously granted its use as the ship's badge for HMCS *Unicorn*. The mythical animal shown in this badge is actually a winged horse, or Pegasus, but having the horn it is transformed into a winged Unicorn. Throughout time, wings have been added to any figure held in veneration. This is as true of angels as it is of Mercury or Pegasus. Looking at its distinguished battle honours, there is every reason why wings should have been added to the unicorn in this badge.

This division was established in Saskatoon, Alberta on November 1, 1941.

Colours White and royal blue

Battle Honours Armada, 1588; Cadiz, 1596; Porto Farina, 1655; Santa Cruz, 1657; Lowestoft, 1655; Orfordness, 1666; Sole Bay, 1672; Schooneveld, 1673; Texel, 1673; "Vestale" 1761; "Tribune" 1796; Basque Roads, 1809; Salerno, 1943; Okinawa, 1945; Korea, 1950-1953.

HMCS York

Blazon *Azure, a white rose of York, rayonne or.*

This badge design was furnished by Admiralty who have graciously granted it use as the ship's badge for HMCS *York*. The cruiser which last wore this name in the RN was abandoned in Suda Bay in May 1941 after being attacked by Italian explosive motor boats. Thus the name was available for the use of the division.

The division was established in Toronto, Ontario on November 1, 1941.

Colours White and azure blue
Motto Bon Espoir (Good hope)
Battle Honours Lowestoft, 1655; Orfordness, 1622; Sole Bay, 1672; Schooneveld, 1673; Texel, 1673; Louisburg, 1758; Martinique, 1809; Atlantic, 1939; Norway, 1940; Mediterranean, 1940-1941; Malta Convoys, 1941.

NAVAL
AIR
SQUADRONS

VX-10 Experimental Air Squadron

Blazon *Argent four aircraft propeller blades in cross azure the lower one resting on a base barry wavy of four azure and argent, over all a saltire couped at the ends fess-wise to represent the letter X gules, in the center of which a small cog-wheel or.*

As this was the experimental air squadron, the X is a rebus on the nature of their operations. The lower propeller blade resting on the heraldic water reinforces the bond between the Navy and the Air arm. The small cog in the very center of the design may have alluded to the fact the squadron was able to keep the wheels of the service turning.

It was formed in March 1953 to test all new aircraft and equipment which entered service with the Navy. The unit is no longer in service.

Colours Red and white
Motto Superbia in progressum

HU-21 Helicopter Utility Squadron

Blazon *Gules, on a base argent and azure of four winged horse courant argent, mane, wings and hoofs gold.*

This squadron was sometimes referred to as the workhorse of the Naval Air Service. Its badge design incorporates the Pegasus, a mythical beast possessed of great strength. It is depicted as if preparing for flight, and the hooves touching the water reaffirm the bond between the squadron and the Navy.

The unit was formed in November 1942 as (VH) Squadron 21 and was renamed HU-21 in April 1955. The unit is no longer in service.

Colours White and red
Motto Omnibus paratus (Prepared for everything)

VU-32 Utility Air Squadron

Blazon *Per fess azure and barry wavy argent and azure, two chain links conjoined in pale, the one in chief argent, the one in base or.*

This badge design illustrates the division between the two environments, the ocean in the lower portion, and the sky in the upper portion. Two chain links demonstrate the bond between the services of sea and air — the Navy and the Air squadron.

The unit was originally the Shearwater Station Squadron Fleet Requirement Unit and was formed in May 1946. It was renamed VH-21 in November 1952 and became a separate squadron on May 2, 1954. Still operational, the squadron flies CT-133 Silver Star jets and CH-135 Twin Huey helicopters.

Colours White and blue

Motto Nihil quam arduam (Nothing too difficult)

VU-33 Utility Air Squadron

Blazon *Per fess azure and barry wavy argent and azure, in chief a chain link palewise argent, pendant therefrom a fouled anchor or, the link passing through the ring of the latter, and upon the chain link, wings displayed and conjoined in base or.*

In the same manner as the badge of VU-32 Squadron, this device shows the two environments of operation — the ocean and the sky. The foul anchor represents units of the navy whilst the upper link in the badge has wings superimposed upon it to indicate its Naval Air affiliation.

This squadron was formed at Patricia Bay, Vancouver Island on November 1, 1954. Still operational, the Squadron files CT-133 Silver Star jets and CP-121 Tracker aircraft from CFB Comox on Vancouver Island.

Colours Gold and blue
Motto Finis coronat opus (The end crowns the deed)

VT-40 Air Training Squadron

Blazon *Azure, in base two bars wavy argent, a comet in the dexter chief with four rays arched in bend or.*

There are several possible interpretations of this squadron badge. In one instance, the comet may symbolize those who rise through training from the sea (in base) to the sky. Another possibility is that the training bestowed by this squadron was the light that guided new people to their destinies — flying over the world's oceans in the service of the crown. It may also be possible that the light from the comet is the heraldic depiction of the skill of the sentinels mentioned in the motto — those who guard ships at sea and provide them with information which is beyond their own horizon.

The squadron was formed in May 1954 and became part of VU-32 in May 1959.

Colours Gold and blue
Motto Ad formandum fatum vigiliarum (To shape the destiny of the sentinels)

HS-50 A/S Helicopter Squadron

Blazon *Or, a base barry wavy azure and argent, a mosquito in flight, probiscus pointed towards and touching the base, proper.*

Here, the insect is poised in the air, its "stinger" probing the waters for its prey. Just as a person is sometimes only aware of a mosquito after it has bitten — so would the submarines be surprised if the squadron unexpectedly struck.

This squadron was formed on July 4, 1955 in Dartmouth, Nova Scotia, but is now no longer operational.

Colours Black and gold
Motto In aure vincimus (By ear we conquer)

404 Maritime Patrol and Training Squadron

Blazon   *A buffalo's head.*

While the official description of the badge is somewhat succinct, it might also be described in a more expanded form as *Argent, a buffalo's head proper, couped and facing to the dexter*. The buffalo's head is used as the main device for this badge because of the reputation of this native of Canada as a fierce and powerful fighter. In its natural habitat, elder members of the buffalo herd will form a barrier between the calves and any predator. This squadron adopts much the same principle, for their fighting capabilities are used to create a barrier — formidable to those who try to attack anything within, and secure to those depending upon it for survival.

This squadron was originally formed as a coastal fighter unit on April 15, 1941 in Thorney Island, Hants, England. It was disbanded on May 15, 1945. The squadron was reformed on April 30, 1951 as a maritime reconnaissance squadron at Greenwood, Nova Scotia, and redesignated maritime patrol on July 17, 1956. Still operational the squadron, VP-404, trains aircrews on the CP-140 Aurora in CFB Greenwood, Nova Scotia.

Motto   Ready to fight
Battle Honours   Atlantic, 1941-1945; English Channel and North Sea, 1941-1945; Biscay, 1943-1944, Normandy, 1944; Baltic, 1944-1945.

164

405 Maritime Patrol Squadron

Blazon *An eagle's head erased faced to the sinister and holding in the beak a sprig of maple.*

This squadron was the first RCAF bomber squadron to go overseas, and was the only RCAF pathfinder squadron. This badge design adopts the eagle's head as its device to suggest leadership, and was an element of the pathfinder badge. This squadron was formed at Driffield, Yorkshire, England on April 23, 1941 and disbanded on September 5, 1945. It was later re-formed as a maritime reconnaissance squadron at Greenwood, Nova Scotia on March 31, 1950, and was redesignated a maritime patrol squadron on July 17, 1956. Still operational, VP-405 flies the CP-140 Aurora from CFB Greenwood, Nova Scotia.

Motto Ducimus (We lead)

Battle Honours Fortress Europe, 1941-1945; France and Germany, 1944-1945; Biscay Ports, 1941-1945; Ruhr, 1941-1945; Berlin, 1941-1945; Normandy, 1944; Biscay 1942-1943.

406 Maritime Operational Training Squadron

Blazon *A lynx salient affrontée.*

This badge design utilizes the lynx as the main device because of its success as a predator. Not only does it have exceptional night vision and tracking capabilities, but it is rarely cheated of a kill. Just as these abilities are handed down from one generation of the cats to the next, this air squadron ensures that a high standard of proficiency is passed from one generation of aircrew to the next.

The squadron was formed as 406 (Night Fighter) Squadron in England on May 10, 1941. It was redesignated 406 (Interceptor) Squadron on November 27, 1944 and disbanded in Cornwall on September 1, 1945. It was later reformed as 406 (TAC B) Squadron (AUX) in Saskatoon on April 1, 1947, then as 406 "City of Saskatoon" Squadron (AUX) on April 1, 1958. The unit was disbanded on April 1, 1964, but later reactivated as HT-406 Squadron. Still operational it trains aircrew on the CH-124 Sea King helicopter at CFB Shearwater, Nova Scotia.

Motto We kill by night

Battle Honours Defence of Britain, 1941-1943; English Channel and North Sea, 1944; Fortress Europe, 1943-1944; France and Germany, 1944-1945; Biscay Ports, 1944; Normandy, 1944; Biscay, 1944.

407 Maritime Patrol Squadron

Blazon   *A winged trident piercing the shank of an anchor.*

This badge represents the blows struck against enemy shipping by the Demon squadron. The trident has cleanly broken the anchor at the exact center of its length suggesting that attacks carried out are not only accurate by deadly.

The squadron was formed as 407 (Coastal Strike) Squadron in Thorney Island, Hants, England on May 8, 1941. Later redesignated 407 (General Reconnaissance) Squadron on January 29, 1943 the squadron was disbanded in Devonshire on June 4, 1945. On July 1, 1952 it was re-formed as a maritime reconnaissance squadron and was redesignated a maritime patrol squadron on July 17, 1956. Still operational, VP-407 flies CP-140 Aurora from CFB Comox, British Columbia.

Motto   To hold on high

Battle Honours   Atlantic, 1943-1945; English Channel and North Sea, 1941-1945; Fortress Europe, 1942; Biscay, 1942-1945; German Ports, 1942; Normandy, 1944.

415 Maritime Patrol Squadron

Blazon   *A swordfish*

The swordfish and motto indicate the squadrons operational duties in the detection and destruction of enemy vessels.

The squadron was formed as 415 (Torpedo Bomber) squadron at Thorney Island, England on August 20, 1941 and disbanded in Yorkshire, England on May 15, 1945. It was later reformed as a maritime patrol squadron in Summerside, Prince Edward Island on May 1, 1961. Still operational, VP-415 flies the CP-140 Aurora from CFB Greenwood, Nova Scotia.

Motto   Ad Metam (To the mark)

Battle Honours   Atlantic, 1942; English Channel and North Sea, 1942-1944; France and Germany, 1944-1945; Biscay, 1942-1943.

423 Helicopter Anti-submarine Squadron

Blazon   *A bald headed eagle volant.*

This badge incorporates the bald eagle as its main device not only because this bird is indigenous to Canada but because of its reputation as a powerful hunter. Its keen eyesight and flying abilities give it great range in its search for prey. When a target is detected, the bird's approach is swift, silent and deadly, fitting qualities for an A/S squadron to emulate.

The squadron was formed as 423 (General Reconnaissance) in Argyll, Scotland on May 18, 1942, and was disbanded in England on September 4, 1945. On June 1, 1953 it was re-formed as 423 All-weather (Fighter) Squadron at St. Hubert, Quebec, but was again disbanded on December 31, 1962 in Grostenquin, France. Now operational and based in CFB Shearwater, HS-423 flies the CH-124 Sea King helicopter from HMC ships.

Motto   Quaerimus et petimus (We search and strike)
Battle Honours   Atlantic, 1942-1945; English Channel and North Sea, 1944-1945; Biscay, 1944.

443 Helicopter Anti-submarine Squadron

Blazon *A hornet affrontée.*

This squadron was known as the Hornet Squadron during World War II, and hence the squadron badge. As anyone who has been stung by one of these insects knows it is a painful and savage attack.

The squadron was formed as 127 (Fighter) Squadron in Dartmouth, Nova Scotia, then renumbered 443 (Fighter) Squadron in Digby, Lincolnshire, England on February 8, 1944. It was disbanded in Utersen, Germany on March 21, 1946 and not reformed until September 15, 1951 in Vancouver, British Columbia. It became the "City of New Westminster" (Fighter) Squadron (AUX) in September, 1952 and disbanded as a fighter squadron on April 1, 1964. Now operational again, HS-443 flies the CH-124 Sea King helicopter from CFB Shearwater in support of maritime operations.

Motto Our sting is death
Battle Honours Fortress Europe, 1944; France and Germany, 1944-1945.

449 Maritime Training Squadron

Blazon *In front of a pomme, a unicorn's head couped.*

This squadron has adopted a unicorn as its badge for, like the creature itself, its abilities are derived from the strengths of the many parts from which it is composed. The *pomme* is in recognition of CFB Greenwood, the location where the new squadron was formed. When the squadron was disbanded its training functions were taken by 404 Squadron.

Motto Unanimi cum ratione (United with a purpose)

VF-870 Naval Air Squadron

Blazon *Azure, out of a base barry wavy of six pieces argent and azure a winged demi lion or, armed and langued gules.*

This badge depicts the lion rising out from the water by means of its wings and assuming a fighting posture.

The squadron was originally one of the Royal Navy Fleet Air Arm, Squadron 803, which had been disbanded in 1944, one of its former members having been Lieutenant Robert Hampton Gray, VC, DSC, RCNVR. Re-formed on June 15, 1945 in Scotland, the squadron became RCN on January 24, 1946, the date of the commissioning of HMCS *Warrior*. On January 15, 1951 she became part of the 19 Support Air Group in Shearwater, and was renumbered VF-870 on May 1, 1951. The unit was disbanded in September, 1962.

Colours White and blue
Motto Intercedimus et delemus (Intercept and destroy)

VF-871 Naval Air Squadron

Blazon   *Azure, a base barry wavy of four argent and azure, over all a winged centaur argent reguardant and arresting, holding in the position to shoot to the sinister a bow and arrow gules, the latter flighted and barbed argent and the bow stringed of the same, a quiver gules filled with arrows and issuing from the dexter side of the centaur, being suspended by a strap or from the sinister shoulder, the centaur winged, armed and unguled or.*

The central device of this badge design is the centaur, but in this instance it has been given wings to assist it as it gallops over the waves of the ocean in search of its enemies. The centaur is shown in the act of stopping, and with the bow in the ready position, as if having sighted a foe, and preparing to attack and destroy it.

Originally Royal Navy Squadron 883 it had been formed at Royal Navy Air Station (RNAS) Yeovilton in October 1941, but was later disbanded and remained inactive until 1945. It became an RCN squadron on January 24, 1946 and joined HMCS *Magnificent* when she commissioned. On May 1, 1951 the squadron was renumbered to 871 and was finally disbanded on March 16, 1959 to amalgamate with VF-870.

Colours   White and red
Motto   Pugnandum surgimus (We rise to fight)

880 Maritime Surveillance Squadron

Blazon *Or, in base three barrulets undy azure, and issuing therefrom a demi-opinicus sable armed and langued gules and holding in the dexter paw a maple leaf of the last.*

The opinicus in this badge is one of the menagerie of heraldic monsters. It resembles a griffin whose upper half is eagle and whose lower half is a lion. The forelegs are those of the lion. It suggests the 880 squadron has the strength of the lion combined with the agility and grace of the eagle. It is seen rising from the sea in response to the call to duty.

This squadron had also been one of the Royal Navy Fleet Air Arm squadrons, (Torpedo-Bomber-Reconnaissance) 825, which had formed in 1934 and served aboard HMS *Eagle*. Disbanded in 1944 it was reactivated as an RCN squadron on July 1, 1945 in preparation for joining HMCS *Warrior* in 1946. It later became part of the 19 Support Air Group, and on May 1, 1951 became part of 880 Squadron. Today MR-880 Squadron flies the CP-121 Tracker aircraft from CFB Summerside, Prince Edward Island.

Colours Black and gold
Motto Reperer et detruire (To seek and to destroy)
Battle Honours Diego Suarez, 1942; North Africa, 1942; Sicily, 1943; Salerno, 1943; Norway, 1944; Japan, 1945.

VS-881 Naval Air Squadron

Blazon *Azure, in base two barrulets undy argent, over all a sword in pale point downwards of the second, pommel and hilt or, enfiling a coronet of Canada of the last, and issuing from behind the sword blade wings conjoined white.*

This badge design follows the basic design of that used by the Royal Navy for their 881 squadron. This design however, incorporates the coronet of Canada.

The squadron was originally formed as Royal Navy Torpedo-Bomber-Reconnaissance 826 in March 1940. Disbanded in 1942 it was briefly recommissioned in between August 1945 and February 1946. The squadron was reactivated on May 15, 1947 as part of 18th Carrier Air Group stationed in Dartmouth, Nova Scotia, and was renumbered 881 Squadron on May 1, 1951. The squadron was amalgamated into VS-880 on July 7, 1959. The squadron is no longer operational.

Colours White and blue
Motto Ense constanter alato (Steadfastly with winged sword)

VC-922 Naval Air Squadron

Blazon   *Barry wavy argent and azure, issuing from the base a demi-sun in splendour and over all a Kwakiutl thunder bird of the west coast Indians, volant and coloured proper.*

This badge design incorporates a background taken from the arms of British Columbia, where the squadron was based, and a creature from Indian folklore. It is depicted in a flying position to represent the air squadron. The squadron was formed on December 1, 1953 as the successor to Cadet Flying Unit 1 and was located in Patricia Bay on Vancouver Island. This unit is no longer operational.

Colours   Gold and black

Motto   Indagando et percutiendo (By tracking and striking)

NAVAL
SHORE
ESTABLISHMENTS

HMCS Albro Lake

Blazon *Barry wavy of twelve argent and azure, a flag argent bordered azure, on which two ship's masts in saltire proper pennants flying inwards argent and in the center over all a torteau from which four lightning flashes pointing outwards, two in vertical position and two horizontal, gules.*

This station's name reflected its former location near the lakes on the northern end of Dartmouth, Nova Scotia, which were named after one of Halifax's early settlers — Mr. John Albro. It was learned that ships of Albro and Company would hoist a merchant's private signal flag (white with a blue border) when entering Halifax harbour. The badge design has been altered by the addition of two ship's masts — a reference to the chandlery business. The disc and the lightning flashes in red are intended to suggest radio and the transmission of messages by that means.

Albro Lake was operating as a Naval Radio Station (NRS) from approximately 1953 until July 1, 1956, at which time she was commissioned as one of HMC NR Stations. She was decommissioned in 1965 and moved to Blandford, Nova Scotia. During the unification of the Armed Forces, the station again changed its name from HMC NRS *Blandford* to Canadian Forces Station (CFS) *Mill Cove*.   ***Colours***   Blue and white

178

HMCS (CFS) Aldergrove

Blazon *Barry wavy of ten argent and azure, a caduceus from the head of which issue three forks of lightning pointing to the dexter, center and sinister chief respectively or, between two alder leaves conjoined on one stem gules.*

The caduceus is the symbol of Hermes, one of the Greek gods. He acted as their herald or messenger. It is used here as a symbol of one who carries, sends or receives messages. The fact that these particular messages are transmitted by means of radio is depicted through the use of the three flashes of lightning that issue forth from the head of the caduceus. The name *Aldergrove* is depicted through the use of a sprig of two alder leaves. These are shown in red because the predominant variety of alder in the location of the radio station is the Red Alder.

Aldergrove was operating as early as November 1943. She became a Naval Radio Station on June 1, 1955 and remained so until commissioning as HMC NRS *Aldergrove* on July 1, 1956. After unification, she was renamed CFS *Aldergrove*.

Colours White and red

HMCS Avalon

Blazon *Argent, a pale engrailed azure charged with a sword in pale point upwards proper, hilt and pommel or garnished with jewels.*

According to the Canadian Board on Geographical Names, there is no record yet discovered that sheds any light on the origin of the name Avalon in Newfoundland. It is, however, mentioned in medieval romance and described as an ocean island, not far on this side of the terrestrial paradise. Avalon was supposed to be the abode of Arthur, Oberon and Morgan le Fay. It was here that Arthur was to have been given his sword Excalibur, which is seen in this badge lying on the deep blue mystery of the sea revealed, as it was to him, by the parting of the mists.

Avalon was originally the shore establishment for the Flag Officer of St. John's Newfoundland. It served as such from May 31, 1951 until July 31, 1956. It was established as an independent accounting establishment by signal, and was never commissioned. The name was then used by a harbourcraft in St. John's. Newfoundland joined Confederation in 1949, and the RCN returned as early as April 5, 1949. It was then commissioned as the headquarters of the SNOIC (Senior Naval Officer in command) on May 1, 1951. The establishment was moved from Buckmaster's Field to the ex-US base at Pepperrell on December 10, 1962, and was finally decommissioned in April 1964.

Colours White and purple

NRS (CFS) Bermuda

Blazon   *Azure, from below the fess point and above an island or, issuant from waves of water argent and vert, two lightning flashes or. In front of the flashes a white tailed tropicbird volant to dexter.*

This station is located on the island of the same name. The badge depicts the white-tailed tropicbird as its main device because it is indigenous to the area, nesting in crevices of the island's cliff faces. Locally, the birds are named longtails.

The rocky island represents Daniel's Head, the physical location of the station. It was originally used as an HF/DF site by the Royal Navy. *Bermuda* operated as a Naval Radio Station from July 1963 until July 1966. After unification, she became CFS *Bermuda*.

Motto   Semper vigilans (Ever watchful)

HMCS *Bytown*

Blazon *Vert, a rudder "ancien" tiller and cheek to the sinister or, charged with a maple leaf gules.*

This naval establishment carried on its strength those responsible for the direction of the Canadian Navy. The use of the heraldic form of a rudder is symbolic of this task of maintaining a course. The use of the red maple leaf indicates, of course, that this is a Canadian establishment, and the green background signifies that it is located ashore.

Bytown was the name of the Naval Headquarters in Ottawa from June 1, 1941 until December 6, 1964. The name was also used for the WRCNS training establishment in Galt Ontario between October 1942 and June 1943. The name here was then changed to *Connestoga*.

Colours Gold and emerald green

HMCS (CFS) Churchill

Blazon *Azure, a wyvern argent, gorged with a naval crown or, and holding in its dexter paw a lightning flash of the third.*

This establishment commemorates the Churchill River which flows into Hudson's Bay. The river was named in honour of John Churchill, first Duke of Marlborough (1650-1722), who was Governor of the Hudson's Bay Company from 1685 to 1691.

The arms of the Marlborough's have wyverns for supporters. These are heraldic monsters, much like a dragon, but with no rear legs. They are usually depicted sitting upright on the tail.

As the station was located at Fort Churchill, Manitoba, the wyvern was used as the reference to the history of the area, but is shown on a blue background, symbolic of the sea, and with the naval crown around its neck. The lightning flashes indicate its function as a radio station.

Churchill was established as a radio station in August 1943. It was commissioned in December 1950 as an HMC NRS, changing in July 1956 to HMCS. It remained so until July 1966. At that time, it was renamed CFS *Churchill*.

Colours White and azure blue
Battle Honours Atlantic, 1941-1944.

HMCS (CFB) Cornwallis

Blazon *Argent, on a mount vert, a cornish chough, wings elevated sable, beaked and legged gules.*

This establishment commemorates the Honourable Edward Cornwallis, first Governor of Nova Scotia from 1749 to 1752. In so doing, a device from his family's arms was used, namely the chough. It was depicted standing on a green mount to signify that this was a shore establishment.

Cornwallis was established in Halifax in May 1942, and was the Naval Training Center until April 1943. It was then moved to Deep Brook, Nova Scotia, where its training functions continued. Upon unification, it was renamed CFB *Cornwallis* and trains all recruits for the three services.

Colours White and black
Motto Learn to serve
Battle Honours Amboina, 1810; China, 1842; Baltic, 1855; Dardanelles, 1915.

HMCS (CFS) *Coverdale*

Blazon *Vert, a cross patonce argent in the center of which a torteau charged with a fouled anchor of the second and between each arm of the cross a wind Or.*

This radio station is named after the community where it is located, Coverdale, New Brunswick. Originally settled by a handful of devout persons, the settlement was named in honour of Miles Coverdale, the great religious reformer who was at one time Bishop of Exeter. Coverdale had been integrally involved in the translation of the Bible into English, and is also credited with the preparation of the Anglican Church's Book of Common Prayer.

In the badge the cross patonce refers to Miles Coverdale, whilst the red disc with golden wings is representative of the old non-substantive badge of Wireless Telegraphy Ratings. Finally, the green field shows that the station is located ashore.

Located near Moncton, New Brunswick, *Coverdale* operated as one of HMC NR Stations from December 1949 until July 1956, when she was commissioned as HMCS *Coverdale*. She continued her work, changing her name to CFS *Coverdale* in July 1966.

Colours White and green
Motto Non deficiunt in vigiliis suis (They never fail in their watches)

HMCS D'Iberville

Blazon *Argent out of a base barry wavy azure and argent, a battlement bridge of three arches proper, masoned sable, within the dexter arch a rose gules slipped and leaved vert, barbed and seeded proper, within the sinister arch a fleur-de-lis azure, and surmounting the bridge an escutcheon of the arms of the Moyne (D'Iberville) viz. azure, three roses 2 and 1 or, with a chief displaying a crescent between two mullers all or.*

This establishment is named after Pierre le Moyne, Sieur D'Iberville, one of the first French naval officers in North America. He had been born in Montreal in 1661. The devices used in this badge design are intended to explain the role that this unit played in the RCN as a bridge between the two official languages of the country — the rose and the fleur-de-lis. The shield is taken from the arms of D'Iberville.

D'Iberville was established as a New Entry training establishment in Quebec City, and was commissioned in October 1952. It continued in this role until it was paid off in July 1961.

Colours Blue and gold
Motto Together — ensemble

HMCS (CFS) Gander

Blazon *Azure, in front of a sun in splendour, a Canada gander rising.*

The badge depicts the namesake of the town in Newfoundland where the radio station is located. The navy blue field denotes its past naval affiliations.

Gander was commissioned as one of HMC Naval Radio Stations in 1957 and remains so today as CFS Gander.

Motto Fidelitas (Steadfastness)

HMCS Gloucester

Blazon *Argent, a chevron gules upon the summit of which a torteau of the same from which issue four lightning flashes azure, two to the dexter and two to the sinister.*

This station was located in Gloucester Township, Ontario which received its name in 1798 in honour of William Frederick, Duke of Gloucester and a nephew of King George II. As a member of the Royal Family, he was entitled to use the arms of the Royal household with his personal badge. As these arms may not be used except by special grant from the sovereign, it was necessary to look for a different inspiration for the badge of this unit. There the chevron and the roundel are taken from the arms of Gloucestershire, England. The later is also the basis of the telegraphists badge and is modified here with the addition of four lightning flashes. These are all placed on a white background in recognition of Canadian colours — red and white.

Colours Red and white
Motto Scientia per disiplinam (Knowledge through discipline)
Battle Honours Lowestoft, 1665; Orfordness, 1666; Sole Bay, 1672; Schooneveld, 1673; Texel, 1673; Ushant, 1747; Jutland, 1916; Calabria, 1940; Matapan, 1940; Crete, 1941; Malta Convoys, 1941; Mediterranean, 1941.

HMCS *Hochelaga*

Blazon *Azure upon a cross of silver birch logs pointed at the ends proper, between the arms of which in saltire, four tridents or, a roundel of the last charged with a log block-house or keep with gallery surrounded by a stockade of logs placed vertically and pointed at the top ends, gules.*

There are two possible translations of the word Hochelaga, one from the Huron-Iroquoian language as *place of beaver dam*, the second is from the Iroquois as a place where one is surprised by an ambuscade. The birch logs with sharpened ends could be appropriate for either of these interpretations, in addition they serve as identifying the functions of *Hochelaga* as a supply centre — a storehouse. The four tridents are for naval affiliation and the gold roundel represents the Island of Montreal. Finally the blockhouse is also a symbol of *Hochelaga*'s function as a supply centre.

Colours Gold and blue

HMCS (CFS) Inuvik

Blazon *Party per pale sable and or, the figure of an Eskimo in native garb argent, embellished azure, his back affrontée and launching with his dexter arm a lightning flash gules.*

This establishment is named for a town in the Northwest Territories. The badge design depicts the seasonally long days and nights. The Inuit figure is symbolic of the northern location of the station, and of the source of the meaning of the word *inuvik*, the place of man. The skill of hunting with a harpoon is depicted here as an attribute of the station in delivery and receipt of messages.

Inuvik was established as one of HMC NR stations on March 12, 1961 although it did not commence operations until March 20. Its predecessor had been HMC NRS *Aklavik*, located in a town of the same name in the Northwest Territories. On September 10, 1963, the station was renamed HMCS *Inuvik*. After unification, she became CFS *Inuvik*.

Colours Yellow and black

Motto Sannaiksemayot sopayanon (Prepared for all things)

Maritime Command

Blazon *Azure, a wooden stocked anchor, foul of its cable, a dexter fluke and sinister stock-arm foremost, debruised by an eagle volant affrontée, the head turned to sinister, all or.*

This command was formed when the Armed Forces were unified. The base of blue is of course, in reference to the oceans of the world where elements of the command can be called upon to operate. The foul anchor has long been the symbol of the navy, and in this badge design represents the naval units of the command. The eagle flying represents the air units of the command. Their close association in the badge design is mimicked in real life for both are essential to successful maritime operations.

Motto Ready aye ready

HMCS *Naden*

Blazon *Or, on a mount vert, a Raven as depicted by the Indians of the North West Coast of America sable, eye, tongue and legs gules.*

This establishment commemorates HMC Schooner *Naden*, which was itself named after the Naden River, the largest river on Graham Island in the Queen Charlotte group. The word naden was used by the Raven Clan of the Haida Indians. It comes from the Indian term *ne dan xada i* meaning Naden River People, a branch of the Ecetas, a family of the Haida Raven Clan.

Originally the Hydrographic Survey Vessel CGS *Naden*, the sailing schooner became tender to the RN College of Canada from June 1918 to June 1920. By November 1922, the name found its way to the Naval Training Establishment in Esquimalt, BC. Here it remained until April 1966 when the forces unified, and *Naden* became part of CFB *Esquimalt*.

Colours Black and emerald green
Motto To teach is to serve

HMCS (CFB) Shearwater

Blazon   *Azure, two barrulets wavy debased argent, and a shearwater volant, proper.*

This establishment commemorates the sloop *Shearwater* which was used as a submarine tender between September 1914 and June 1919. The name was then used to rename the RCAF Station at Dartmouth, Nova Scotia, which became HMCS *Shearwater* on December 1,1948. It remained so until the unification of the armed forces when it became CFB *Shearwater*.

Colours   White and azure blue
Motto   Supra mare volamus (We fly over the sea)
Battle Honours   North Sea, 1940-1945.

HMCS (CFS) Shelburne

Blazon *Azure, a pegasus rampant, bridled, crined and unguled or, the wings addorsed and inverted of the same, charged upon the shoulder with a fleur-de-lis of the field and holding between the forelegs an étoile gold.*

The town of Shelburne in Nova Scotia was settled by United Empire Loyalists in 1783. With respect for the Shelburne family coat of arms, the present badge uses the pegasus and the polar star from this source.

Shelburne was originally the Headquarters for the NOIC and associated Naval establishment located there between May 1942 and January 31, 1946. In April 1955 it became a joint RCN-USN oceanographic station. It was renamed after unification to CFS *Shelburne*.

Colours White and blue
Motto Serving in silence

HMCS Stadacona

Blazon *Azure, a sinister arm couped at the shoulder and embowed vambraced argent, the hand armed and grasping an ancient lamp or, flammant proper.*

Since the name was first introduced into the RCN in 1915, units bearing the name *Stadacona* have played many parts. However, by far the most important of these was the training which she undertook to achieve. This fact is incorporated into the badge design, for on the field of blue representing the ocean, an arm holding the lamp of knowledge is shown.

Stadacona was officially established as the Naval Training unit on July 1, 1923. She remained so until April 1, 1966. After unification, she became part of what is now CFB *Halifax*.

Colours White and royal blue
Motto By wisdom and valour

HMCS *Venture*

Blazon *Barry wavy argent and azure on which a pile of the first fimbriated or, charged with a maple leaf gules bearing a naval crown or, sails argent.*

In the design of this badge, the oceans of the world are depicted heraldically as a field of wavy white and blue lines. The V-shape is a symbol of growth and also the bow of a ship ploughing through the water.

While the name *Venture* has been used by several vessels in the RCN, it is perhaps most recognizable as the name of the Junior Officer Training Establishment which was commissioned on August 11, 1954. The training center was paid off when the forces were unified. In September 1976, the Officer Training Division of Fleet School Esquimalt was established, and was moved into HMC Dockyard to the old *Venture* complex in 1977. Today, as part of Training Group Pacific, it is known as *Venture* — the Naval Officer Training Center.

Colours Gold and blue

Glossary of Heraldic Terms

accolée   side by side — especially of two shields

addorsed   back to back

affrontée   a beast or object placed so as to show its full front to the viewer

annulet   a ring

appaumé   of an open hand or gauntlet when showing the palm

argent   silver

armed   concerning claws, horns, talons, and teeth of birds, beasts and monsters

arms   strictly speaking applies only to the charges, the design borne on a shield; often freely used when referring to the complete armorial achievement

attired   bearing antlers

attires   antlers of a stag

augmentation   an honourable addition to the armorial insignia

azure   blue

bar   a narrow horizontal ordinary narrower than a fess

barbed   having the leaf-like sepals which appear between the petals of the heraldic rose

barrulet   a narrow bar

barry   division of the field into an even number of horizontal pieces

barwise   of charges placed horizontally and one above the other

bend   an ordinary formed by two diagonal lines from dexter chief to sinister base

bend sinister,in   following the line of a bend (running from sinister chief to dexter base).

bendlet   the diminutive of the bend

bezant   a gold roundlet (circular object) supposed to have been derived from Byzantine coins

caboshed   of an animal's head affrontée, cut off and showing no part of the neck

canton   a rectangle in dexter chief less than a quarter of the shield

cartouche   an oval shape having the long axis palewise

charge   any object or figure placed on an heraldic shield or comprising part of an armorial composition

chevron   an heraldic ordinary, an inverted V, one third of the width of the shield

chevronel   term for two or more chevrons borne on a shield

chief   an ordinary formed by a horizontal line so as to contain the uppermost part of the shield

cotises   the second diminutive of the bend, and a quarter the width of the shield

couped   cut, cut short evenly

courant   running

crescent   a charge in the form of a stylized crescent moon

cresset   a beacon

crined   describing the colour of hair or mane

cross patée   having the limbs splayed and with straight ends

debruised   see *surmounted*

defamed   a beast deprived of a tail

demi   halved (the upper or front half)

dexter   the right-hand side of shield from the point of view of the person behind it, and so the left-hand side to the viewer

difference   to add to or vary pre-existing arms so as to achieve distinctiveness for one reason or another

displayed   with wings extended

ducal coronet   a coronet of four strawberry leaves (three visible)

elevated   raised, of wings of birds,etc

embowed   bent, curved as a bow

enfiled   encircled

engrailed   of ornamental line dividing a shield into parts or outlining a figure on a shield, comprising repeated semi-circles with points outwards

ensigned   having insignia (i.e. a crown or coronet) placed above it

eradicated   of a tree or plant having been pulled by force from the ground

erased   torn off and leaving a ragged edge

ermine   fur with black tails on white

escutcheon   shield

extended   stretched out

fess   an ordinary comprising a broad band placed horizontally across a shield and occupying about one third of the total area.

fesswise   horizontal

field   the background or surface of a shield and the like upon which the armorial design is shown

fillet   a diminutive of the chief — a narrow bend, one quarter of the chief in depth

fimbriated   a narrow border usually on a cross

flanches   space enclosed by an arc — one on each side dividing the shield into three parts

fusil   a diamond-shaped figure narrow in its minor axis representing a spindle

galley   an ancient ship for both sailing and rowing, shown with one mast unless otherwise blazoned

garb   a sheaf of cereal or grain

gorged   encircled round the throat or neck

gorged, ducally   the throat or neck encircled by a ducal coronet

goutté de larmes   drops of tears

griffin   an heraldic monster comprising head, breast, wings and forelegs like those of an eagle with the hindquarters and tail of as lion. Also *segreant*

guardant   of a beast with its head turned so as to face the viewer

gules   red

hauriant   of a fish, placed vertically with head upwards

helm   protective metal armour for head and neck to the crown of which the crest is secured

invected   complementary to *engrailed*, being the same line of semi-circles conjoined but applied in opposition

issuant   proceeding out or from

langued   concerning the colour of the tongue of a creature

lozenge   a diamond-shaped figure

lymphad   see *galley*

martlet   an heraldic swallow-bird represented as having feather tufts at the end of its legs but no feet

mullet   five-pointed star

mural crown   a crown in the form of an embattled wall

naval crown   a circlet upon which are mounted alternately the stems and sails of ships

or   gold

ordinary   one of the earliest forms of heraldic device; geometric shapes such as the chevron, chief, pale, fess, bend, plain cross throughout, etc

orle   a border in the same form as the shield

pale   an ordinary formed by two vertical lines containing the central part of the shield

pale, in   of a number of objects as occupying the position of a pale, as in the arms of England

pall   a figure resembling the letter y

paly   a design comprising an equal number of vertical stripes or pallets coloured alternately

party   field is divided

passant   walking, of a beast

Pegasus   a winged horse

pheon   barbed head of an arrow engrailed on the inner side of the barbs

pierced   with a round hole in the center showing the field or some other tincture

pile   a wedge shaped figure which issues from the chief

plate   a silver roundel

proper   in natural or normal colours

purpure   purple

rampant   of a beast, with one hind paw on the ground, and the other three raised, the tail erect with the beast looking to its front

reguardant   of a charge, with the head turned so as to look backwards over the shoulder

roundel   a flat, circular object

sable   black

salient   attacking and leaping upon

saltire   a diagonal cross in the form of an x

saltire, per   following the line of a saltire

seeded   specifically for an heraldic rose but also applicable to other flowers when the central disc differs in colour from the flower itself

sejant   seated

seme   strewn with any charge

seme-de-lis   strewn with fleurs-de-lis

sinister   left side of shield from the point of view of the person behind it, and so the right side of the viewer

slipped   of a flower, leaf or twig when it has the stem by which it was attached to the parent stem or plant

statant   of a beast, standing having all four paws on the ground and facing to the dexter unless otherwise stated

surmounted   of a charge, having another charge placed over it (also *debruised*)

tinctures   the two metals (or and argent), seven colours (azure, gules, sable, vert, purpure, tenne [orange], murrey or sanguine [reddish purple]), and two furs of the ermine and vair patterns

torteau   a roundel

trefoil   a stylized leaf with three lobes, usually slipped

tressure   a narrow band inset from the edge of the shield, usually double

undy   wavy

unguled   of an animal having hoofs

unicorn   heraldic creature with the head and body of a horse, one long horn projecting from the forehead, cloven hoofs, a lion's tail, tufted hocks and a beard

vair   an heraldic fur which represents the belly and back skins of the grey squirrel

vambraced   an arm in plate armour, hand gauntleted and usually clenched

vert   green

volant   flying

wavy   undulating, of a line dividing a shield into parts or outlining a figure placed on a shield

wyvern   a fictitious beast with a dog-like head, a horn on the snout, a bird-like neck, and scales instead of feathers on the breast, a snake-like tail, curling, terminating in a barb, with legs of an eagle, a pair of monstrous wings and a protruding, barbed tongue. It is symbolic of malice

Complete list of badges in this book

Commander Canadian Fleet
Badge of the Canadian Navy

HMC Ships

HMCS Acadia
HMCS Algonquin
HMCS Annapolis
HMCS Antigonish
HMCS Assiniboine
HMCS Athabascan
HMCS Beacon Hill
HMCS Beaver
HMCS Blue Heron
HMCS Bluethroat
HMCS Bonaventure
HMCS Bras D'Or
HMCS Brockville
HMCS Buckingham
HMCS Cap de la Madeleine
HMCS Cape Breton
HMCS Cape Scott
HMCS Caribou
HMCS Cayuga
HMCS Cedarwood
HMCS Chaleur
HMCS Chaudière
HMCS Chignecto
HMCS Columbia
HMCS Comox
HMCS Cordova
HMCS Cormorant
HMCS Cougar
HMCS Cowichan
HMCS Crescent
HMCS Crusader
HMCS Digby
HMCS Elk
HMCS Fort Erie
HMCS Fort Frances
HMCS Fortune
HMCS Fraser
HMCS Fundy
HMCS Gaspe

HMCS Gatineau
HMCS Granby
HMCS Grilse
HMCS Haida
HMCS Halifax
HMCS Huron
HMCS Inch Arran
HMCS Iroquois
HMCS James Bay
HMCS Jonquière
HMCS Kapuskasing
HMCS Kootenay
HMCS La Hulloise
HMCS Labrador
HMCS Lanark
HMCS Lauzon
HMCS Llewellyn
HMCS Lloyd George
HMCS Loon
HMCS Mackenzie
HMCS Magnificent
HMCS Mallard
HMCS Margaree
HMCS Micmac
HMCS Minas
HMCS Miramichi
HMCS Moose
HMCS New Glasgow
HMCS New Liskeard
HMCS New Waterford
HMCS Niagara
HMCS Niobe
HMCS Nipigon
HMCS Nootka
HMCS Ojibwa
HMCS Okanagan
HMCS Onondaga
HMCS Ontario
HMCS Oriole

HMCS Oshawa
HMCS Ottawa
HMCS Outremont
HMCS Penetang
HMCS Portage
HMCS Porte Dauphine
HMCS Porte de la Reine
HMCS Porte Quebec
HMCS Porte Saint Jean
HMCS Porte Saint-Louis
HMCS Preserver
HMCS Prestonian
HMCS Protecteur
HMCS Provider
HMCS Qu'Appelle
HMCS Quebec
HMCS Quinte
HMCS Raccoon
HMCS Rainbow
HMCS Resolute
HMCS Restigouche
HMCS Revelstone
HMCS Rockcliffe
HMCS Saguenay
HMCS St. Anthony
HMCS St. Charles
HMCS St. Croix
HMCS St. John
HMCS St. Laurent
HMCS St. Stephen
HMCS Ste. Therese
HMCS Sasketchewan
HMCS Sault Ste Marie
HMCS Sioux
HMCS Skeena
HMCS Stettler
HMCS Sussexvale
HMCS Swansea

HMCS Terra Nova
HMCS Thunder
HMCS Toronto
HMCS Trinity
HMCS Ungava
HMCS Victoriaville
HMCS Wallaceburg
HMCS Warrior
HMCS Whitethroat
HMCS Winnipeg
HMCS Wolf
HMCS Yukon

Reserve Divisions

HMCS Brunswicker
HMCS Cabot
HMCS Carleton
HMCS Cataraqui
HMCS Chatham
HMCS Chippawa
HMCS Discovery
HMCS Donnacona
HMCS Griffon
HMCS Hunter
HMCS Malahat
HMCS Montcalm
HMCS Nonsuch
HMCS Patriot
HMCS Prevost
HMCS Quadra
HMCS Queen
HMCS Queen Charlotte
HMCS Scotian
HMCS Star
HMCS Tecumseh
HMCS Unicorn
HMCS York

Naval Air Squadrons

VX — 10 Experimental Air Squadron
HU — 21 Utility Helicopter Squadron
VU 32 Utility Air Squadron
VU — 33 Utility Air Squadron
VT — 40 Air Training Squadron
HS — 50 A/S Helicopter Squadron
404 Maritime Training Squadron
405 Maritime Patrol Squadron
406 Maritime Operational Training Squadron

407 Maritime Patrol Squadron
415 Maritime Patrol Squadron
423 Helicopter Anti-Submarine Squadron
443 Helicopter Anti-Submarine Squadron
449 Maritime Training Squadron
VF — 870 Naval Air Squadron
VF 871 Naval Air Squadron
880 Maritime Surveillance Squadron
VS — 881 Air Squadron
VC 922 Naval Air Squadron

Naval Shore Establishments

HMCS Albro Lake
HMCS (CFS) Aldergrove
HMCS Avalon
NRS (CFS) Bermuda
HMCS Bytown
HMCS (CFS) Churchill
HMCS (CFS) Cornwallis
HMCS (CFS) Coverdale
HMCS D'Iberville
HMCS (CFS) Gander
HMCS Gloucester
HMCS Hochelaga
HMCS Inuvik
Maritime Command
HMCS Naden
HMCS (CFB) Shearwater
HMCS (CFS) Shelburne
HMCS Stadacona
HMCS Venture